WRITING ON LOVE, KINDNESS & EMPATHY

MY HEART & SOUL

Unplugged

LORNA RAMIREZ

Published in Australia by ?

First published in Australia 2024
This edition published 2024
Copyright © Lorna Ramirez 2024
Cover design, typesetting: WorkingType (www.workingtype.com.au)

The right of Lorna Ramirez to be identified as the
Author of the Work has been asserted in accordance with the
Copyright, Designs and Patents Act 1988.

All rights reserved. No part of this publication may be reproduced, stored in a retrieval system, or transmitted, in any form or by any means without the prior written permission of the publisher, nor be otherwise circulated in any form of binding or cover other than that in which it is published and without a similar condition being imposed on the subsequent purchaser.

ISBN:
Paperback: 978-0-6452197-0-8
Ebook: 978-0-6452197-1-5

About the Author

Lorna Ramirez is a writer, published author of seven books, the latest is *My Heart and Soul Unplugged*, published three Ghost writing books. She is also a publisher, motivational speaker, ghost writer, a pianist and a regular contributor of *The Philippine Times* and the *Philippine Community Herald newspaper.*

She finished her Chemical Engineering degree at the University of Santo Tomas, Philippines and had worked as a Laboratory and Mill Manager at a textile industry in the Philippines. Lorna has travelled extensively, gaining much from her interactions with people all over the world and building strong foundations for her philosophies in life. She loves gardening, cooking and playing the piano both classical and modern.

In 1977, with her husband and her son and her daughter she migrated to Australia. She worked as a Lab Technician in Monsanto and was the first female to ever been employed by the company. Then she worked as an Industrial Chemist in one of the leading oil companies in Australia after her degree in Chemical Engineering was recognised in Australia, only retiring in the year 2000 to care for her first grandchild.

Lorna Ramirez won third prize for the 2017 writing competition by the Society of Women Writers in Victoria. In 2016, Lorna was one of the certificate of recognition award recipients from the Filipino Community Council of Australia (FILCCA). Lorna was voted one of the five most inspiring Women of Australia in 2019 by the Women's Association Incorporated. In 2020 she was recognised as one of the two most inspiring woman by the Skylark Foundation in Australia.

She is a financial supporter of different charities, National Breast Cancer Foundation and to the different Church dioceses in the western suburbs Victoria. Her future project in mind is the writing of the sequel from her novel Moments of Love, Lust and Ecstasy, a cookbook, and another book for inspirational messages, original poems and quotes.

Lorna is often invited to different libraries in Victoria to speak about writing and encouraging young would be writers on how to publish their written manuscript

Throughout her life, Lorna Ramirez, a woman of faith, has been a wise observer of human behaviour and has collected and many wisdoms and observations to produce these inspiring and uplifting books

This book is dedicated to:
My supportive and loving husband, Claro
Grandchildren, Alyssa and Amelia
Children and their partners:
Carlo and Marie
Maria and Steve
To my sisters:
Victoria and Myrna

Acknowledgements

Special Thanks to my daughter Maria Cary in helping me to produce this inspiring book.

Special Thanks also to *The Philippine Times Melbourne*, for publishing my advertisement and my articles.

Preface

This book is a collection of articles I had written and were published at the *Philippine Times* Melbourne newspaper and at the *Sydney Community Herald*. This book is my original written poem, inspirational messages and quotes. Any similarities to other writings are purely coincidental.

My love and close bonding with my families, loved ones and friends and my strong connection with GOD had inspired me to write all the beautiful passages and inspirational messages.

I do hope the readers will enjoy as well as relate to the topics and sensitive issues that were presented in this book *My Heart and soul unplugged*.

Lorna Ramirez

Contents

Preface		viii
1	Finding Happiness	1
2	The Song of Love	6
3	Peace Within	10
4	The Pathway of Life	14
5	Remembering Your Roots	18
6	The Very Essence of Christmas	22
7	Sea Change	26
8	Love Hurts	30
9	The Pain and Joy of Giving	34
10	The Art of Lying	38
11	Grief Turning to Joy	42
12	Empathy, Love, and Kindness	46
13	Life is Worth Living	50
14	Self-Isolation	54
15	Larger Than Life…My Dad	58
16	Pen is Mightier than the Sword	62
17	The Path to Freedom	66
18	Lenten Season Holiest Week of the Year	70
19	Grieving With The Loss of Your Loved One	74
20	My Special Stella Cherry Tree	78
21	The Day I Called Australia Home	81

22	What I Learned From Covid	86
23	For the Love of God	90
24	Welcome … The Autumn Season	94
25	Mother Dearest	98
26	Diverticulitis Awareness	101
27	Dad … The Hero	105
28	Planning To Retire?	108
29	Thanks for the Memories	112
30	Miracles Do Exist	115
31	Forgiveness as a Virtue	118
32	Mother's Unconditional Love	120
33	It's All About Love	124
34	What's in a Dream	128
35	The Spirit of Christmas	133
Quotes and Inspirational Messages		137

1
Finding Happiness

Whilst the pandemic created havoc, tears, and heartaches around the world, we realised now that our lives had changed. Perseverance, vigilance, being cautious in the way we live is the new normal. Indeed, we appreciate more the importance of health, families, and friends.

This pandemic opened my eyes on all the things I took for granted. Thanks for this pandemic I was able to re-assess my priorities in life. I abhor all the excesses of all the material things I once so desired pre pandemic. I learn to live and enjoy simple things in life, and I am happier now more than ever.

I had given up all the material things I possessed, like expensive jewelleries, bag, shoes, garments to my family and some were donated to charity. Pre pandemic, I went to Crown Casino once a week spending money. I thought I was happy and enjoying life at that time. It is almost three years I had never played at Crown Casino and to my surprise I am not really missing it.

DEFINING HAPPINESS

Happiness for me is doing what I love:

Happiness, I feel each time I cook delicious dishes for my

grandchildren, and watching them eat with gusto, the food I prepared with love.

I found happiness nurturing and caring for my plants, doing gardening with my husband, looking after our veggie's patch, fruit trees, and many flowering species at the backyard.

Happiness for me is tickling the ivory keys, playing classical pieces hence triggering a powerful emotional sense that enable me to express what the composer wants to convey in his piece.

Reading a novel or an inspirational book will always make me happy

Happiness is just sitting beside my hubby at night sipping coffee or tea while watching a movie or listening to beautiful oldies songs in the 60's or 70's. Simple as it is but for me it is contentment and sheer pleasure sharing special moments with the love of my life.

Happiness is going out visiting loved ones, long driving with hubby, visiting beautiful places with him but with proper mask for protection.

I found solace, comfort, and happiness praying, and connecting with Him.

Happiness is giving and supporting worthy charitable organisations in Australia as well as some of our Filipino organisations.

The year 2022 was a dreadful and positive year for me. I lost some of my investments, but on the positive side, year 2022 my brain aneurysm had stabilised, the blood vessel in my brain had shrunk according to the latest MRI test. So happy for the result. It was in the year 2022, my gastroenterologist specialist had discovered that the Aspirin I had taken for years was causing my bleeding and assured me I won't be having any more bleeding episodes. Alhough I lost a substantial amount of money in the year 2022, I am still grateful that all my health issues were all resolved. AS I always say.... Health is more important than money and power!!

Lastly, I want to share a beautiful quote from one of my favourite authors "Bishop Fulton Sheen"

"Joy is the happiness of love.... Love is aware of its own inner happiness

Pleasure comes from without, and joy comes from within, and it is therefore within reach".

An excerpt from my book *Reflective Contemplation*

HAPPINESS

Happy are those who can forgive.

Because they will find peace

Within and others

Happy are those who stay connected.

With HIM

It's the only way to eternal salvation

Happy are those who are willing to share

And help others.

Because they make a difference

In this troubled world

We live in

Happy are those who can love.

And accept people.

Because they will be able to love and beloved

2

The Song of Love

Why do we get easily hurt when we love someone? Why is it when egregious behaviour was manifested by loved ones, we easily responded to their emotions? Why is it we are very sensitive, when we love someone so dearly? I believe the answer is that when we are in love, we are so emotionally connected to a person we adore and cherish, hence the expectation from our beloved is at its highest level, making us so effusive and sentimental that even frivolous words and actions by them, can be interpreted in a negative way and hurting us intensely. Indeed, we can be too sensitive and overreact for no reason at all.

Love is akin to the air we breathe that sustains our lives, yet we cannot see it. Love is something too profound to be felt in our hearts and souls but invisible to the human eye. Love can be potent, can also be an inspiration. Overall love is truly magical.

Music is one of the many examples in expressing our love to someone. The most beautiful melodies are all a declaration of our undying love to a person. Most people who listen to love songs can relate to their innermost feelings. Music and love are so connected that they complement one another. Songs of love can arouse your emotions and can bring back wonderful memories of years gone by.

2 The Song of Love

Music is an expression of love. Lovers have their theme songs. Countries, clubs, organisations all have their songs that symbolise love, patriotism, and loyalty.

One of my most enjoyable moments is listening to the 60's and 70's love songs at night with my husband, sipping tea or coffee at our family room, reminiscing our younger days and all the beautiful memories and experiences we had gone through. Listening to love songs evoke nostalgic moments thus creating a sense of strong connection between my husband and me.

Love and music can inspire us to be the best of what we are. A McGill University study cited by the Psychology Today from the Science of Music and Love written by Noah Kest, breaks down how music can cause a release of Dopamine in the brain, "the fuel good chemical" is usually released, when listening to love songs.

Music most especially love songs can heal our pain, and at times help us go through difficult times of our lives. Love songs can alleviate your loneliness when someone you love is on the other side of the globe and beyond your reach.

All of us love the melody of love songs composed by well-known composers and musicians. However, when we had gone through heartaches, frustrations, and disappointments, the melody of the songs become irrelevant. The lyrics of the love songs will be more important than the actual melody, because the frustrated lover can relate more to the lyrics of the "SONG OF LOVE", thus making the song of love to be his or her "THE SONG OF LIFE."

Excerpts from my book *Reflective Contemplations:*

THE POWER OF LOVE

Love encompasses everything.

Does not know its boundaries.

It is so strong and powerful.

It will conquer everything.

Along its path

Does not care who you are.

Regardless of gender, status, beliefs or religions

Makes a strong man cry.

And a weak man strong.

3

Peace Within

"Unless souls are saved, nothing is saved, there can be no peace unless there is soul peace". This is a remarkable opening line by Bishop Fulton Sheen in one of his books. A grim reminder of what is happening now in the world. Wars are created by people with conflicts in their soul, no peace within, and instead greed and power are their ultimate goals. As St. Augustine said, "The root of sins is pride" Some prominent leaders in the world want to show that they are strong and powerful, then pride and greed had taken control of their minds and spirits, hence doing the unthinkable and making decision that will create fear and anxiety globally.

Dread arises because being human we are aware of the danger around us, and it touches our very souls and spirits, producing anxiety complex in our present civilization.

If we throw a stone into a pond, it will create a ripple effect, akin to the pandemic that created devastation and depredation on the entire world. Tsunami of mental illnesses, depression occurred. Peace of mind, and fear affected most of us. We have not fully recovered from the impact of Pandemic another challenge for the humanity eventuated. Russia invaded Ukraine, an unprovoked attacked without any valid reasons. Security, peace of the nations will be at stake, and the possibility of a cataclysmic world war, that we all hope won't happen. This is a conundrum situation to the European nations, the US, and all the democratic nations in the world. Then again greed, power, and pride prevail by a leader who wants to show that he is strong and powerful. I do not think he has peace within his soul. If he fails with his ambition, his actions will haunt him forever and he will become the opprobrium of the world and his country will be a pariah state. Is it all worth it? Only time will tell.

TWO KINDS OF WEALTH

According to Bishop Fulton Sheen, there are two kinds of wealth

NATURAL WEALTH

Takes the form of necessary food, clothing, and shelter to sustain life of an individual and family. It is possible for a person to satisfy his natural wealth because his stomach can consume only a limited amount of food once it reaches the saturation point.

ARTIFICIAL WEALTH

Consist of money, credit, stocks, bonds, and the rest of the material things. With the artificial wealth, the satisfaction is insatiable. The determination to amass more wealth will be the main focused, hence deprivation of inner peace will prevail. When this artificial wealth started to crumble and fade away, it will lead to desperation, anxiety. The soul can be lost and confused and peace within will be unattainable.

CONCLUSION

I believe most of us are guilty of the excesses of the present time. We are all victims of materialism. One of the positive aspects of the pandemic for me, is the realisation of what is important and the reassessment of my priorities in my life. There is nothing wrong to enjoy the modern luxuries in life, but at times it becomes an obsession that will lead to frustrations. You can never be satisfied and wanting for more. I accumulated so much material things, shoes, jewelleries, bags, dresses that I realised not of vital importance for me now. How did I come to this? Luckily, I have granddaughter, daughter to dispose all of these. I found myself happier now doing spiritual contemplation, by reading, meditation and finding inner peace within. I also believe you must have peace within to have peace with others. Lastly please reflect and digest the meaning of this saying from the bible,

MARK 8:36

WHAT DOES IT PROFIT A MAN TO GAIN THE WHOLE WORLD YET FORFEIT HIS SOUL?

Excerpt from my book *The Realities of Life*

Demons' monsters, evil are very true
Yet we cannot see them
Because they are lurking within us
Fight and conquer them we must
For if we fail
Eventually they will poison and overtake
Our body, mind, and soul

4
The Pathway of Life

The season of the year is akin to the cycles of life or the pathway of life. The spring symbolises new beginning, new life, like a newborn child that is full of hope and aspiration. Then comes summer season. Vibrant, warm, and radiant. Trees, shrubs, and flowers are in full bloom. In humans, they are in the peak of their success. Wealth and power are their ultimate goals and enjoying life to the fullest.

During autumn, trees start to shed their leaves. Flowers stop blooming. For us humans, we start to mellow. We see life in different perspectives. We are more forgiving, compassionate, and less aggressive. At this stage we are planning our future in retirement.

As expected, when winter comes, plants and trees will be dormant or hibernating. In humans we are reaching the end of our journey. And this is what I call the twilight years of our lives.

Twilight years of life
Twilight years of life are not all doom and gloom. At times this is an enjoyable stage of life, with no responsibility of parenthood. Especially if you have financial freedom, you can focus on things

that you enjoy doing. You can start chasing your passions. My husband and I are enjoying our retirement pursuing doing things we love. In my twilight years of life, I made a crucial decision, to make a total right knee replacement surgery. Hence, the saga has started.

Knee replacement surgery

I was admitted to a private hospital in March this year for a right knee replacement surgery, not knowing the consequences that may arise. The average recovery of knee surgery is about three to six months. However, it can take up to twelve months for full recovery.

Waking up after the surgery, I found that anaesthesia had affected me immensely. I started vomiting, and my throat was numb for a day, not able to swallow nor eat. This problem was resolved the following day as the anaesthesia wore off. I stayed at the hospital for four days, then transferred to the hospital rehabilitation ward where I stayed for ten days. The rehabilitation was intense. We were to do physio exercised morning and afternoon for almost an hour each session. The pain during the exercise was unbearable, even worse than childbirth. The physio exercises are necessary to strengthen the knee's muscle and improve range of motion, and to be able to resume your independence. Throughout my stay at the hospital, I was injected with blood thinning drugs to avoid the risk of blood clots after surgery. I raised my concern to the doctor, that any thinning drugs would cause abdominal bleeding, to which the doctor explained that it is needed. Without it, I run the risk of having fatal blood clots. I hesitantly obliged.

Hospital discharge

I was discharged after fourteen days. The doctor gave me another batch of tablets of blood thinning drugs, to be taken twice a day for seven days. I continue my rehabilitation at home. After two weeks I had intestinal bleeding. I was rushed to another hospital, where my colorectal surgeon is based. The bleeding stopped after four days, and I was discharged. Just after a week at home another problem came about. I had an excruciating abdominal pain and found myself back at the hospital. My specialist decided to do a series of tests, gastroscopy, several blood tests, CAT scan, and ultrasound. The ultrasound will detect the flow of blood vessels to check of any blockages in my intestine. There were no abnormalities detected. My specialist and his team of colorectal surgeons concluded that the thinning drugs plus the strong morphine given to me after the surgery were the contributing factors for my bleeding and unsettled stomach. One of the specialists recommended for me to try the FODMAP diet, eliminating garlic, onion, and some fruits and veggies with high FODMAP. Optimistically, my stomach will return to normality post-surgery in a few months' time. I'm doing well now and can walk without any walking aids just five weeks after surgery.

Despite all these hurdles, I don't have any regrets. At times we are stronger than we think. Being focused, staying positive, and determination to succeed are the best way to overcome problems along the way.

I do wish that my experiences would not deter anyone thinking of doing this major operation. Any operation will have a risk, but at times taking a risk has its own reward... Life is such a gamble!

Excerpt from my book – *Reflective Contemplation*

The season of winter is akin to the darkest moment of our lives. Unforeseen traumatic tragedies will happen. If you have a solid faith in God and support of loved ones and friends, you can overcome all your predicaments. Soon spring will be around. New hope, new beginning. Our journey will be rosier and more joyful than ever.

5

Remembering Your Roots

"He who does not know how to look where they came from, will never get to his destination" This is one of the popular quotes by Dr. Jose Rizal. Dr. Jose Rizal is considered as the greatest Filipino hero, thus earning him the title as the Philippine's national hero.

Wherever we go, especially migrating to country of your choice, for seeking greener pastures, we should always remember our roots. We are still Filipino in flesh and blood and in heart and soul.

The first few years that we migrated to Australia with my family in the late 70's, we started missing the culture, cuisines, friends, and relations that we left behind. To alleviate our loneliness, we bonded with other Filipino families. We continued to practice our culture, celebrating Christmas and New year with our extended families here in Australia. Unfortunately, in the 70's there are no Filo restaurants and groceries in Melbourne, thus homesickness prevailed.

As years passed, we became more involved and busier with our work and raising our children. Teaching and introducing the heritage and culture of our motherland were forgotten. My children now all married can understand but cannot speak the language, more so with my two granddaughters who cannot understand the dialect. My granddaughters now are blaming me that I should had done more, teaching them the language, and the culture of my homeland.

In our younger days, we travelled extensively around the world, except the Philippines. It took us forty years to finally visited my homeland, then I realised what we had missed. My youngest 18-year-old granddaughter loves Filo cuisines, and I am currently giving her lessons cooking authentic Filipino dishes.

Nowadays with the influx of Filo students and migrants from the Philippines, the Filipino culture is more alive and vibrant. We now have so many Filipino restaurants, festivities and so many events sponsored by different Filipino Communities and organisations.

DIFFERENT WAYS CONNECTING TO OUR ROOTS

Just like the roots in a tree, the roots provided nourishment and growth to the branches. Strong roots provide healthy branches and strong produce. Teaching your children, the values and culture of their roots will make them strong and make them well grounded. In my opinion the following are the different ways to connect to our roots.

1. Try hard to teach them to speak the language where you came from. Another popular quote by Dr. Jose Rizal "He who does not love his own language is worse than an animal and smelly fish.

2. Emphasise to your children the values and heritage of your roots.
3. Encourage them to visit the place where you came from, to enhance their knowledge of how ordinary people live, their values and culture.
4. Introduce them the taste of different Filipino cuisines at an early age.
5. Encourage them to attend and possibly participate Filipino festivities and events.
6. Give them books to read about the Philippines or watch Filipino movies.
7. Motivate them to mingle with Filipino group, hence they can learn a lot of their roots.
8. Inspire them to buy and appreciate the Filipino products.

It is indeed of utmost importance not to forget where you came from. Knowing your history and heritage will increase your knowledge of yourself and what you are now. The connection from your past should never be taken for granted, and the importance of your heritage is of great value. It should be passed on to the future generations. Being in my twilight years of life, I realised I should had done more; however, it is not too late yet. As the saying goes....... It is better late than never.

Excerpt from my book *Pondering Thoughts*

What is a secret of a successful person?

They always remain humble.

And they don't forget their roots.

And the people who helped them

6

The Very Essence of Christmas

I believe that the true essence of Christmas will be Love, Forgiveness and Humility. Jesus exemplified all these virtues. HE was born in a manger, an epitome manifestation of humility. HE died on the cross to redeem us from sin certainly an act of love to all mankind. Forgiveness was mentioned on HIS first and second last words when HE was crucified. The first word; Father forgive them, for they know not what they do and the second words; Today you will be with me in paradise.

Even in the popular Lord's Prayer recited by all Christians around the globe, forgiveness was also mentioned. This Christmas, let us all have time to reflect, meditate, and do soul searching. Christmas should be a time for preparation for our spiritual upliftment. To nourish our body and soul, by doing good deeds and helping those who need the most. We should spare a thought for those who can't celebrate with their families; example are the expatriates and all OFW (Overseas-Filipino Workers) the soldiers overseas in their mission for peace. The sick and the lonely. For some people Christmas is a time of sorrow, some parents do not have the means to buy presents for their children.

Only then we realised how lucky we are that we can afford and manage to celebrate this important festive season with all our loved ones and friends.

Christmas is a very special event for Christians, celebrating and remembering the birth of Christ. For most of us, it is the time of parties, merrymaking, gorging of food and alcohol and the anticipation of that long-awaited holiday. The church will be busy preparing for Christmas with the beginning of advent in late November and culminating till the 24th of December. For us Filipinos we will be attending Simbang Gabi (Night-Mass) which begins on the 16th of December and ends on Christmas eve, 24th of December

Most houses during Christmas season will be decorated with lights. Tall Christmas Trees packed with gifts, Christmas Stockings hanging at the wall, the children waiting for Saint Nicholas to fill it up on Christmas Day will be found in every house. Parents will be spending lavish gifts for their children. There will be lots of careful preparation for the food on Christmas Day. There is nothing wrong with these. It is a Christmas tradition for bonding with families and friends. Joyful moments experienced by all during Christmas celebration.

With all these festivities are we forgetting the real essence of Christmas? Are we more consumed and focused on material things and ourselves? I think we all are. I believe it is not too late to do the change, we can practice the virtues of Love, Forgiveness and Humility. It will be a challenge for us, but it can be done.

HAPPY CHRISTMAS TO ALL AND GOD BLESS

Excerpt from my book *Reflective Contemplations*

Happiness
Happy are those who can forgive
Because they will find peace
Within and others
Happy are those who stay connected with HIM
It is the only way to eternal-salvation
Happy are those who are willing to share
And help others
Because they can make a difference
In this troubled world we live in
Happy are those who can love
And accept people
Because they will be able to love and be loved

7

Sea Change

Goodbye 2020 and say hello to 2021. What lessons have we learned from 2020 during COVID 19? Perhaps in 2021, a change will be needed for a new perspective and aspiration in life. Perhaps most of us now realised that health and family are the most important things in life.

This Pandemic in 2020 gave havoc and economic destructions globally and we are one of the lucky few countries to be able to control the virus, thanks for the bipartisan cooperation of both political parties we can control this virulent and horrible virus. Australians too should be congratulated for being vigilant and adhering to the rules imposed by our government.

People who lost loved ones and grieving, should begin to move on and start afresh. They must remember and be aware that there are still living loved ones around them.

Hackneyed old saying's "life is too short" that is often used in messages, songs, poems and everyday conversations, is a relevant phrase for welcoming the new year of 2021. This is the time to be brave enough to get out from your comfort zone because life is too short to be doing nothing and at times change is needed for a better tomorrow.

I believe welcoming the new year is the time for" SEA CHANGE".

7 Sea Change

What is sea change? It is a significant change in one's lifestyle or a profound transformation of a person. Sea change will also depend upon your priorities in life. If you want to be healthy in 2021, change to a healthy lifestyle by minimising the consumption of alcohol, junk foods, and be courageous and determined enough to stop smoking.

Sea change can also be a change of career, to follow and chasing your passion and pursue whatever your heart desires. I started going back to taking piano lessons in my late 60's and I am hoping to pass my last year intermediate grade 8 piano exam by AMEB (Australian Music Examination Board) by next year. As a retired industrial chemist by trade, I started writing only five years ago and never looked back. These are the perfect examples that age is not a hindrance in pursuing your dreams.

For empty nester, it is a life changing experience and a big decision for them to either downsize or to move from city to the countryside, hence enjoying their retiring years. Whatever decisions you will be making for the year ahead it should be for the best of yourself and loved ones.

If you want to make a difference in the year 2021, you can start doing community services and helping, reaching and sharing to those people who are less fortunate than us. It will not only give you a sense of satisfaction in what you are doing but you will have peace within yourself, knowing that you are able to help people even in the smallest possible way and that to me is PRICELESS.

Challenge yourself and make plans for the year ahead. Please remember what you do now will have a great impact in your life in the future HAPPY NEW YEAR TO ALL

Excerpt from my book *The Realities Of Life*

CHANGE

Change means courage, discipline

Change means humility

Acceptance of your fault and inadequacies

Change means enlightenment

The truth revealed

Change means aspiring

To do the right things at the right time

Take one step at a time

With sheer determination

You can be a better person

Now than before

7 Sea Change

8

Love Hurts

"You always hurt the one you love, the one you should not hurt at all". This is the opening of the song Hurt, a song popularised by Timi Yuro, a soul singer of the 60's era. This is one of my favourite songs of all time. This song encapsulated what love is, and how we are sensitive when loving someone with all our heart.

Why do we get easily hurt, once we loved someone? So many answers for this question, but in my opinion one of the main reasons for this is that we are so emotionally attached to the person we adore and expectation to someone we loved is at its highest level. Even frivolous words and actions portrayed by loved ones can be interpreted as hurting by the recipient, indeed we can be too sensitive and overreact for no reasons at all.

Why is it when egregious behaviour is manifested by loved ones, we easily react to their emotions but cannot tolerate others for doing so? Because we care and always protect those we love.

People in love usually have an inexorable attitude. They won't be persuaded and blinded by the truth. Love is so potent it can change a person. It makes a strong man cries and a weak man strong. Love can destroy families and friends and even divide nations. It can strike you anytime, anywhere without warning. Such a mystical power of love.

Loving is not easy, it has its perils, however one can also experience the joy, happiness, contentment and inspiration of a person truly in love. Love can also kill. One can die of a broken heart, called a broken heart syndrome. Women are more prone than men to experience this kind of syndrome. Even in the animal kingdom, we can witness this kind of syndrome. A good example is my rabbit. Two baby rabbits were given to us by my grandchildren last Christmas in 2018. We cared and nurtured both. Their names were Aly and Amy, and after six months Aly was able to dig a hole and free herself. We never found her. Amy had shown a sign of depression missing her companion rabbit. She did not eat for two days, and we were worried. We gave Amy attention and tender loving care by feeding her manually, and only slowly she responded and get back to normal.

There are those people who can't move on, especially a mother losing her child. The love of a mother to her children is beyond measure and hard to fathom. My friend in America had lost her only child. She did not recover from the tragedy. She succumbed to depression until her husband left him which led her to take her own life. Love is beyond comprehension, no one will find the answers to how and why do we fall in love. It is really a mystery beyond the concept of science.

As the ending of the lyrics of the song HURT says," So if I broke your heart last night. It is because I love you most of all." A valid reason to say for your loved ones if you hurt them!

Excerpts from my book *Reflective Contemplations*

Finding Love

Being in love we start to

Rediscover our inner self

And the real meaning of what life is all about

Finding love is magical

Moments and precious time

We shared with someone

We truly love and adore

Finding love is priceless

8 Love Hurts

9

The Pain and Joy of Giving

The popular adage of "**IT IS BETTER TO GIVE THAN TO RECEIVE**" is now fully manifested in this once in a century pandemic. With the furlough of thousands of front line and health workers, it had created strain in our health system especially in age care and hospitals throughout the country.

Health workers do not have a choice but to work double shifts thus resulting of being overworked, exhausted yet they continue to give due care for people affected with COVID. Deep in their hearts they found joy in serving those who are sick and the most vulnerable people in our society. However, they always felt the pain each time holding the hands of a dying patient and seeing tears flowing from their face crying and longing to be near their loved ones. Such a sorrowful scenario to be witnessed by anyone.

A young niece of mine had recently graduated and now work as a nurse in one of the hospitals in Australia is the paradigm of how young people sacrifice enjoying the prime of their youth but instead found themselves in a difficult situation witnessing the havoc of this pandemic it had created. There are times my niece came home with tears in her eyes lamented that watching her patient gasping for breath and yet she cannot do anything more but only give comforting words and remain at their bedside up to their last breath is the only thing she can offer. For sure most of nurses experiencing this situation will be affected mentally, emotionally, and physically. I told my niece to remain strong and focus and she replied that even with the grim situation she is encountering daily, she is also happy that she can make a difference and added that it had opened her eyes and realise the importance of her job as a nurse.

It is always enthralling every time I hear stories of bravery, dedication and especially the selfless devotion of our health workers for caring the sick not only COVID but with other ailments and diseases.

It is true that this pandemic brings out the best in us but unfortunately it also highlighted the ugly side of us. There are people who will make money out of the misery of others. There are retailers who will sell the RAT (Rapid Antigen Test) at an exorbitant price that is out of reach for the impoverished people in our society. So sad that this is happening in Australia.

Another archetype of how people will display their passion and love of giving are the soldiers, missionaries, charity workers and the list can go on and on. These soldiers are happy that they can serve the country, the missionaries are happy to spread the words of God and the charity workers found fulfilment helping the needy and the poor. All of them at times feel the pain to be away from their loved ones, sacrificing their time, and feel the pain involve of risking their lives doing the jobs they are passionate of. Not to forget as well are those parents who will give everything, they can to give their children the best care and education. When the children decided to leave, they found themselves an empty nester and the pain to be alone is too much to bear especially if their children had forgotten them.

Because of our love and passion to give as much as we can, we should always be prepared to accept the consequences and the aftermath of the pain of loving and giving, indeed this is the HARSH REALITIES OF LIFE!

Excerpt from my book *Reflective Contemplations*

Angels do not need wings
You can be an angel
By reaching and helping others
Each one of us can make a difference

9 The Pain and Joy of Giving

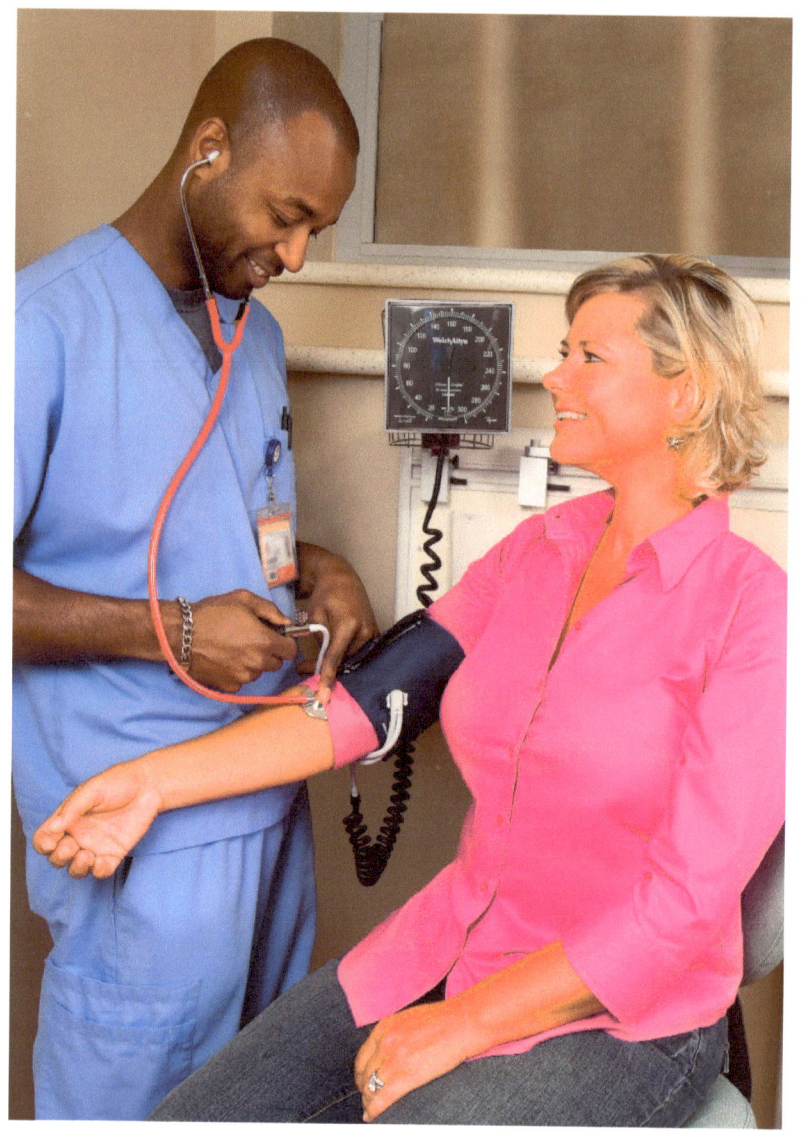

10
The Art of Lying

All of us had lied once or many times in our lives, however there are people who cannot help themselves by lying all the time. These are the pathological liars. This is also known as Mythomania and Pseudologia Fantastica, a mental condition affecting the nervous system. A person with this condition will be inclined to lie all the time, unfortunately, these people will be ending up believing their own lies thus they are detaching from reality and cannot distinguish between fact and fiction

COLOURS OF LIES

White Lie White lies are usually not harmful. A person will do it to protect loved ones from hurt and miseries

Gray lie Almost the same as white lie but the only difference is partly to help oneself and gain benefit out of it. At times it will be difficult to differentiate it with white lie

Black Lie This is a selfish lie. People will lie to get themselves out of trouble and not responsible for their action.

Red Lie This is the worst of all lies. A person will lie to harm others out of revenge for those who had wronged them. They will destroy a person integrity and seek pleasure to destroy them morally, and emotionally. This is indeed a horrible side of human character.

Sometimes we are blindsided from the people we trusted, especially coming from loved ones, family friends and most of the time by the government. Their lies often changed our perspective in life thus affecting our judgement and can be detrimental to our future and our journey of life. The lies often will create heartaches, mental confusion and at some instances the loss of lives.

Due to the success and the popularity of social media such as Twitter, Facebook, Instagram, and other forms of social communications lies can easily be expanded, resulting to the existence of Conspiracy Theories, an outlandish exploitation of lies hence creating chaos and misinformation within the wider community. At the end people will be perplexed knowing the truth from lies.

Because of this, people will not trust the media, journalists and will be in disillusion of whom to trust. This is sad but it is happening in some part of the world. We are so lucky in Australia we do not succumb yet to this kind of environment. We still have a faith on our political- system and I can proudly say we are so lucky living in Australia.

WHY DO WE LIE

Same as children, adults lie to avoid punishment and responsibility for their actions

People lie for their self-preservation, to feed their ego and also will lie to attain success and achieve their dreams,

Some people will lie to get the merit and reward they desperately want

We lie to protect our loved ones. A sacrifice worth doing

At times we lie to be polite and trying not to embarrass another person

The list will go on and on. One must remember lying is a human instinct. Whether they are good or bad lies these lies will be forever with us THROUGH ETERNITY.

Excerpt from my book *My Passion My Calling*

Honesty and being truthful

Begin first in oneself

Before it can fully

Transcend to others

Sounds simple but difficult

Especially when one's ego

Will be affected

11

Grief Turning to Joy

The intensity of grief cannot be denied hence it will affect people in many-different ways. Grief will come in many forms, but the utmost level of grief is the loss of someone you loved. There are more than five million of deaths and counting because of this Pandemic. For those who have lost loved ones, most will be scarred for life and be left with gaping hole in their hearts. For some they moved on and found peace within.

It is indeed unfortunate that there are minority of people gaslighting the validity and the reality of Covid 19 and these people are questioning the effectivity of the wearing of mask and social-distancing. I believe this is one of the many reasons that lead to the explosion of this one in a century pandemic. Elucidating these people to see the truth is futile since they were already brain washed by some social media outlets that promote misinformation and conspiracy theorists. They are now of a diminishing flock of unbelievers.

Grief created by this pandemic, is turning into joy and hope, when several vaccines are now available to combat this pandemic ravaging all over the globe. We will succeed at the end!

There are so many life experiences that can cause grief, such as loss of job, career failure, marriage or relationship breakdown, financial difficulties to name a few. In spite all these predicaments in life there are those who manage to get through, and conquer their problems, hence their grief turned to joy and success. They emerged stronger and a better person than ever.

I was grief stricken last year of 2020. At the heights of the pandemic, lockdown and isolation in Melbourne, I had internal bleeding and was rushed to the hospital. It was a nightmare, not knowing when my bleeding will stop thus putting a lot of anxiety from my loved ones. I had several blood transfusions, and when I was about to be operated my bleeding stopped. I stayed at the hospital for almost fourteen days.

As I was recuperating at home, I had a bad fall resulting the damaged cartilage at my right knee I can hardly walk but decided not to go to the hospital due to Covid 19. I was depressed and miserable since I can't hug my grandchildren and children and that was so painful for me. Because of the isolation I had depression slowly seeping within. I lost interest and passion to write and tickle my ivory keys. I was so fortunate that with support of my husband and our family doctor, I slowly recovered and now on the mend. With the easing of restrictions is a big relief and helped me in my recovery. Now I started again doing what I love to do; writing, my music, cooking gardening and enjoying precious moments with my loved. My grief turned into joy Once again I do appreciate what life is all about. I also firmly believe that life experiences will make you stronger and serve as an inspiration to do better next time around

As the saying goes.........THERE WILL ALWAYS BE A LIGHT AT THE END OF THE TUNNEL

Excerpt from my book *My Innermost Thoughts*

SUFFERING IN SILENCE

At times we cry within

Yet no one can hear

The pain and hurt, only you can feel

Those shattered dreams and memories of yester-years

That haunt you vividly as only they can

But that was then and today is different

Years have passed and things have changed

Once again, triumphantly now you emerge

A better stronger person

11 Grief Turning to Joy

12

Empathy, Love, and Kindness

CHARACTER MATTERS......A phrase we often hear these days. Why does character matters. I am sure most of you will agree that the character of a person is an imperative aspect or force of leadership be it in politics, businesses, communities, and charitable organisations.

Indeed, the character of a person will define who you are, hence it is often called, The Mirror of Your Soul. Your character will have a tremendous influence in the choices and decisions you will be making, and hopefully the right pathway for success.

I firmly believe that to have righteousness and integrity, you should possess these virtues of empathy, love, and kindness. The confluence of these virtues will be the embodiment and one of the basic formations of a good moral character of a person.

For further enlightenment, these are the descriptions of the following virtues:

EMPATHY

The ability to understand and share the feelings and emotions of people, empathy can be an emotional, thought, or compassionate. It is a feeling of someone's pain and ready to help and do something about it.

LOVE

This is a universal feeling. It is inherent for us to love our families, relations, and friends, but love goes beyond these. We should also love others that do not share our sentiments and convictions.

KINDNESS

It is the quality of being friendly and considerate and not judgemental. It is a virtue of helping others who are needing the most without expecting anything in returns. Kindness is treating people as they are, regardless of race, belief, and gender.

Can someone be kind without empathy? Of course, yes, you can help people with their predicaments, but you do not empathise, especially if that person was responsible for their own problems they created. At times, some people will digress from their shortcomings, and blaming others for their mistakes, obviously an ugly side of the character of a person.

This is one good example of why character matters, our high school valedictorian, was a very smart person, but lacking in social skills, and the art of interacting with people. He has no empathy nor kindness in his heart. He topped the board exams in Chemical engineering in the Philippines as well in the US. Five years ago, we had a high school reunion in California, and saddened to hear he was a failure in his career and cannot keep a permanent job.

There are lots of anger, hatred, greed, love of power in the world. If we have all these virtuous of empathy, love, and kindness in our hearts, I believe this world will be a better place to live!

Excerpt from my book… My Innermost Thoughts

It is with giving that we find the joy of sharing.

It is in loving that we can fully feel how it is to be loved

It is in understanding that we can practise the art of compassion

It is in believing in ourselves that we can focus and do

Anything our hearts desire. It is in trusting in HIM

That we can find the inspirations and courage to do all these things

12   Empathy, Love, and Kindness

13

Reasons That Life is Worth Living

It is often you read this hackneyed old saying that "Life is Worth Living" which is used by many songwriters' writers, authors, and laypersons as an expression of their perspective analysis of life. It is indeed a very interesting topic worth discussing and reflecting

Each of us has our own journey of life. A journey we must overcome all trepidations and challenges along the way. At times we are besieged with problems, and we started to be confused, and begin thinking of the gloom and doom of the world around us, hence a sign of developing mental problem. Few years ago, I nearly succumb to this path of uncertainty and fortunately I soon realised that these are the four reasons that changed my life and happy to say that "LIFE IS WORTH LIVING"

A. CONNECTION WITH GOD

If you have a strong relationship with "HIM" you know that you are not alone in your journey. Your faith in "HIM" will give you the inner strength to fight and be strong. Through prayers You can connect and find peace within. Thomas Merton, a priest monk, and a spiritual writer said "To seek God perfectly is to withdraw from illusion and pleasure, from the worldly anxieties and desires from the works that God does not want, from the glory that is, only human display". We are obsessed with power, wealth material things in this world. and success hence we are disconnected with reality, thus seeing ourselves superior to others. They don't need God, at the end when things had gone wrong, they begin to despair, falling to the dark pit of obstacles in life. If we could only practice half of Thomas Merton said, I believe we can lead a positive life and see the world a beautiful place to live.

B. LOVED ONES

Children's laughter, noisy feet of small children playing in the room, especially from your Children and grandchildren will always bring joy, and smile to everyone. Connecting with Friends and enjoying moments with them sharing beautiful memories with one another, are the many reasons why life is worth living. Indeed, loving someone has its own rewards.

C. CHASING AND FOLLOWING YOUR DREAM

Life will be monotonous and meaningless without goals and purpose in life. Stephen Benet, American poet and novelist said in one of his books "Life is not lost by dying, life is lost minute by minute, day by dragging day in all thousand small uncaring ways" Very true Indeed, time will be wasted by doing nothing. Chase your destiny, explore your potentials and soon you will perceive that is life interesting and worth living. There are people in the
   Twilight years of life being very successful by discovering their

potentials. Frank McCourt Started writing at the age of 62, he wrote Angela's Ashes that won him both the Pulitzer Prize and the National Critics Circle Award. I started writing in my 70's and to date had published six books and three Ghost Writing books. There are people who find purpose in life by joining community activities, with the goal of helping those who are needing the most and being active in many charitable activities

D. THE BEAUTY OF NATURE

When I was a little girl, I asked my mother the reason why there was a rainbow in the sky and my mom said, "it is a miracle in the sky". Until now I always gaze in awe each time a rainbow appears in the sky. I do appreciate now more than ever the beautiful dazzling colours of flowers, from different varieties of plants especially the breathtaking colours of roses. You must look around, and witness the beautiful creations bestowed upon us.

All these things I mentioned above gave me the reason to smile and appreciate all the blessings I do have. As the saying goes "SMILE AND THE WORLD SMILES WITH YOU, CRY AND YOU CRY ALONE"

Excerpt from my book *The Realities Of Life*

LOVING YOUR LIFE

Love the life you live

Appreciate the things you have

Be it small or big, wake up each day with enthusiasm

Full of hope and determination that today

Will be better than yesterday

Make tomorrow another day of joy and bliss

14

Self- Isolation

MEANING OF SELF-ISOLATION

This is an act of voluntarily isolating oneself from others, due to fear, depression, or other reasons perceived by the person.

It is without a shadow of doubt that the pandemic in 2020 created and started this problem. Unfortunately, I chose to self-isolate. I was paranoid and fearful of catching COVID or other viruses. I refrained from visiting shopping centres, groceries, banking, and places where there are group of people to be encountered. It was a blessing that my husband did all these for me.

Limiting the visitations of loved ones and stopped socialising with close friends and acquaintances were difficult to bear and put a dent in my heart. I remained calm, firm, and make myself busy doing things I love; cooking, writing, tickling the ivory keys, reading, and exercises. I did not go through depression and anxiety, but I can feel deep within something is missing hence I decided to come out from my shell.

January of this year 2023, a friend invited me to attend an outdoor event celebrating Australia Day by one of the major Filipino organisations. I was taken aback, loud music, big crowd and I almost passed out. My friend encouraged and helped me dealing with the situation. I am taking baby steps and slowly interacting with friends.

WHAT ARE THE SIGNS OF SELF ISOLATION
1. Spending time to be alone and avoiding social interaction.
2. Experiencing panic or anxiety seeing large group of people
3. Limiting your social contact with family and friends
4. Always cancelling plans and make excuses not to mingle with friends.
5. Being always paranoid of getting infected being with people
6. Lack of social skills due to self-isolating
7. Deterioration of self confidence

AFTERMATH OF SELF-ISOLATION
A study by an epidemiologist at the New Castle University concluded that deficiency in social relationship is associated with higher risk of coronary heart disease and stroke.

According to the Australian Government Institute of Health and Science Isolation can be harmful to our mental and physical health and well-being.

All health experts agree that self-isolation will affect your self-esteem, resulting to depression and anxiety

In my opinion, I believe that losing your sense of connection with society, will change your perspective of the world around you, hence affecting you emotionally, physically, and mentally.

HOW TO OVERCOME SELF-ISOLATION

1. Self determination to change is the main aspect to overcome self-isolation.
2. Reach out to your family and friends and discuss your problems.
3. Be active in social media such email, voice call and text.
4. Seek help or talk to your family doctor about your problem.
5. Read, research, and understand the implication of self-isolation.
6. Be busy, develop interest in other fields, you will be surprised to discover your talent.

Is my self-isolation worth it? Yes and no. Yes, because until now I am COVID free. No because I missed my interactions with family and friends. I am confident I can put everything behind me and start a new life of freedom and free from fear of the unknown. The starting line of the poem of John Donne's Devotion said, "No man is an island entire of itself". An expression so true it struck a chord with me thus reminding me that PEOPLE NEED PEOPLE TO HAVE A NORMAL WAY OF LIFE!

Excerpt from my book *The Realities of Life*

Change means courage, discipline

Change means humility

Accepting of your fault and inadequacies

Change means enlightenment

The truth revealed.

Change means aspiring

To do the right thing at the right time

Take one step at a time.

With sheer determination

You can be a better person

Than before!

15

Larger Than Life...My Dad

Every Father's Day, I always feel the pain in my heart because I am missing my beloved Dad. My Dad's legacy lives on forever. His generosity is second to none. During his living years, he had helped his brothers and sisters and my mom's brothers and sisters to pursue their dreams of finishing their university degrees in Manila. My dad had touched so many lives. He was a person who will give his last money in his pocket to someone needing help. A remarkable person in many ways. His kindness, generosity resonate with us his three daughters.

I can still remember his beautiful infectious smile that is crisp and warm as the morning sun. His laughter was akin to the sound of the mighty roaring seas. Every time he was with loved ones and friends, his eyes will sparkle like the stars in the sky, a truly a vision of happiness. He really loved to be with people and in returned he was loved and respected by everybody who knew him.

Being a father is not an easy job. Fathers tried to always remain strong, but deep within, they do have a soft spot for their children especially their daughters. We can always persuade Dad to give us things we asked for, but unfortunately Mom will always say no. In some difficult situation, Dad remained cool, calm, and strong thus gaining our respect and we idolised him as our hero.

My Dad's kindness, unconditional love, generosity, and joyous nature have a big impact in all my writings. Thank you, Dad, for making me what I am today. You will always be in my heart forever.

FATHERS OF YESTERDAY VERSUS FATHERS OF TODAY
Fathers of yesterday were a distant figure, while fathers of today are expected to help with the care and upbringing of their children, because we are busier now than before, and our children are always involved in many social activities such as swimming, sports, and music lessons.

In the past, fathers were supposed to be the prime bread winner, but today's fathers are happy to be a stay-at-home dad looking after their children while their wives who have the higher incomes are working and bringing home the bacon.

In the past fathers were the disciplinarian but today, mothers have an input on how to discipline her children.

Today's father can communicate freely with their children and their children have more freedom to talk to their fathers which in the past was not possible.

Fathers in the past do not get involved with their children's activities, they were solely the bread winner of the family. Nowadays fathers love to be involved in all their children's activities.

Despite these differences, there is one thing in common for both the fathers of today and yesterday, they always make sure to protect their families from all unexpected events and predicaments. They will always sacrifice anything for the sake of their families.

Regardless of the situations, fathers will love and take care of their families.

It is of paramount importance to celebrate Father's Day not only for the month of September but all year round to give them recognition for their role as the FATHER OF THE FAMILY.

To all fathers....... HAPPY FATHERS DAY

Excerpt from my book *Chasing My Passion, and my Calling*

> Through the eyes of the children
> Their parents are their role models and heroes.
> Therefore, it is the responsibility
> Of every parent to set high standards
> To be able to produce
> Future responsible adults

15 Larger Than Life...My Dad

16

Pen is Mightier than the Sword

This is a popular adage, first written by the novelist and playwright writer Edward Bulwer-Lytton in 1839. This is true indeed in many aspects of life. Written words can pierce through your heart and soul and at times can be nestled deeply forever in your heart, while a knife that pierce in your skin can heal overtime. A paradigm of what the mighty pen can do while the sword can't achieve. The pen can destroy a person morally, spiritually, mentally and can drive a person to insanity.

The Philippine's national hero Dr Jose Rizal had written literary master pieces to arouse people's love for the country as well as exposing abuses by the Spanish government and Spanish priests. In today's environment, so many writers were persecuted because they were using the pen to spread the truth. Nowadays the social media replaces the pen as the way of communications. There are times people using them for bullying, misinformation and promoting conspiracy theories. On the positive side we have so many self-help and inspirational books that can change the mindset and increase positive thinking of the readers.

I had written several Inspirational books that had touched the lives of the reader. Here are some of the positive feedback I received.

HOW MY BOOKS IMPACTED SOME PEOPLE'S LIVES

1. I received an email from someone who was a battered wife. Before going to bed and upon waking up in the morning she would read my inspirational book to be able for her to deal with her difficult situation for the day. By reading my book she had gained self-confidence and the courage to leave her abusive husband. She was thanking me to have given her the inspiration, self-esteem, and was able to see life in a different perspective.

2. A friend of mine who had a friend with terminal cancer bought my first book" The Realities of Life". He gave the book to his dying friend. It was emotionally moving when my friend informed me that his dying friend loved the book. He said he was not afraid of dying anymore and he treated each day as a blessing. Reading the book had given him strength to face death fearlessly.

3. I was at the Doctors clinic, and I was discussing my inspirational books to my friend. An elderly person who heard that I was an author, had requested if he could buy my book. So lucky I had a spare book in my car, and I also gave him my phone number in case he needed help. One Sunday morning I received a call from him. He was thanking me that the book had touched him immensely. He was living by himself, and the wife had passed away few months ago. My book gave him determination and power to face life and cope with his loneliness. Since then, he had purchased the rest of my published books.

4. Someone from a regional area had also given me positive feedback about my book. She even implored to pray for her because she was having personal conflict. I gladly obliged, however I explained to her that I had also my flaws just like the rest of us. She replied" In my eyes you are my hero and an angel on earth. ". Wow I was so humbled.
5. The mother of a friend of mine said that her mom was loving so much my book that she was reading it repeatedly.
6. These are some of the feedback I received but to me they were truly special and priceless. It is indeed an author's dream to be able to relate and touch the hearts and souls of their readers. I am so thrilled I am successful in achieving these.

Excerpts from my book *Pondering Thoughts*.

Do not underestimate the power of words.

The Power of Writing

It can do more harm than you ever realise.

It can destroy a person's reputation.

17

The Path to Freedom

Franklin D. Roosevelt said "In the truest sense, freedom cannot be bestowed. It must be achieved." This is precisely true indeed. Freedom must be earned. We should be responsible for our future. You have the freedom to make a choice, the right path to succeed, to look after your health, finances, and relationship to create your future for a better tomorrow.

We should be looking forward and embrace the new year, with full of positivity, and enthusiasm, to change bad habits from the previous year. Consider each coming year as a new beginning. Free yourself from all the heartaches, frustrations from past year and make these experiences as your guide and strength to face new challenges in the coming years.

We should not forever be a prisoner of our self. It is up to us to relinquish the past, let it go and move on. Failing to do so, peace within can never be found.

I am sure most of us will come up with goals and plans to do the New Year resolution for each year. We must remember that changes cannot be done overnight. It should be done one step at a time. We must evaluate, contemplate of what is the most important aspect in your life you want to change. Work on that with sheer determination, discipline, and focus so you can achieve and conquer it.

It is no use of having a long list of New Year resolutions. The Forbes Health/ one poll survey (from google) found that the average resolution last 3.74 months. Only 8% of respondent tend to stick with the goals for one month, 22% last two months and 13% last four months. Nonetheless, remember that the choices you made will create and shape your future, reassessing your inner self is the best way to start. Begin with the easy part that is achievable then do one step at a time. The following are my ideas to have an effective New Year's resolution:

HOW TO ACHIEVE YOUR GOALS FOR YOUR NEW YEAR RESOLUTIONS

1. Be rational, know what is achievable and what is impossible.
2. Do your planning or strategy how to do it.
3. Analyse what is your priority in life that you want to change.
4. Be focus and have strong determination to do it.
5. Set a realistic goal and work on it.
6. Do small steps at a time until you succeed and then proceed to the next goal.
7. Do not be discouraged failing, start all over again this time more determined than ever!
8. Consider your loved ones when making changes, and how it will affect them.

Of course, change is inevitable, circumstances will change as we go to the different stages of life, this is a part of our journey in life. However, as I always asserted, change and humility are two words that go hand in hand. Humility is the acceptance of the mistakes we made from the previous year and change is the courage to correct it. With these in mind, you will be ready to have a new path of freedom and welcome each year with peace within and peace with others.

I believe that the best thing in life is free, and life is not worth living without inner peace and FREEDOM.

Excerpt from my book *Realities of Life*

SPECIAL MOMENTS

Each special moment

Has that special meaning

That will be forever, embedded in our hearts.

Each challenge and endeavour

We have gone through.

Needs patience, hope and perseverance.

From each failure and mistake we had

Lessons can be learned.

Can be used as an inspiration.

To start all over again

Till we achieve our dreams

18

Lenten Season Holiest Week of the Year

Palm Sunday is the beginning of Holy Week. This is the entry of Jesus and all his disciples into Jerusalem, greeted by people waving palm branches. This is celebrated by all Christian churches all over the world.

HOLY WEEK CELEBRATIONS AROUND THE WORLD

The church mourns for the death of Christ and different countries have their own celebrations for Holy Week.

PHILIPPINES

In the Philippines there is a re-enactment of the final days of Christ before his crucifixion. There are eight people in rural areas that re-enacted the actual crucifixion of Christ on a Good Friday. However, the Catholic Church discourage these unnecessary sacrifices.

Self-Flagellation… Done to make amends for sins. It is practice by flogging your back with whips for repentance of sins. Led by Pope Clement VI, the Catholic Church does not approve self-flagellation.

Senakulo…. One of the widespread traditions in playing Jesus's life during Holy Week. This is mostly observed in the provinces of San Pedro Pampanga and Paombong Bulacan. It is performed on a stage or on a street for several nights during the Lenten season.

Pabasa This features an uninterrupted singing and reciting the passion of Christ from the verses of the bible from three consecutive days and nights.

Station of the Cross ... Done on Good Friday, then at 3:00 pm churches will have Good Friday services for the commemoration of the passion of Christ and His seven Last words before He died on the cross.

Easter Sunday This is called Pasko Ng Pagkabuhay "the resurrection of Christ". Families bonded together for the feast celebrations while the kids enjoy Easter Egg hunting.

AUSTRALIA

Good Friday and Easter Monday are national public holidays in Australia. The religious people will perform rituals, such as fasting, prayers, and attending special church services and long prayer vigils. For less religious minded people, they take advantage of the long weekend and plan their holiday trip. Hot cross buns are the most popular easter staple by many Australians. Egg hunt is the most popular game during Easter celebration with the family.

KENYA

In Kenya Holy Week is celebrated by Christians attending the church every day for four days and ending in Easter Sunday. On Good Friday they have processions, re- enactment of the Stations of the cross. On Easter Sunday they will say "Heri Kwa Sikukuu

Ya Pasaka" meaning" Blessed be the Passover Feast". Easter Sunday Families will stay together feasting and celebrating the resurrection of Christ

ISRAEL

Many people believe that this is the best place to celebrate the Holy Week, by visiting the Holy Land. Thousands of pilgrims will visit Jerusalem at the Holy Sepulchre. A mass of the Last Supper is celebrated on Holy Thursday. At night there will be a holy hour at the garden of Gethsemane. There will be a procession a procession at the church of St. Peter in Galli Cantu. At the Calvary on Good Friday the Lord's Passion and crucifixion will be remembered, then the station of the cross will follow. The climax of the celebrations will end on Easter Vigil on a Saturday. A mass is celebrated on Easter Sunday with a procession around Christ tomb.

These are only some of the countries that Christians all over the world are celebrating the holiest week of the year...... The Lenten Season

REFLECTIONS

Holy week is the time of contemplations and evaluations of inner self. This is the time for prayers, fasting, repentance, almsgiving, and love. We should reflect that this is the time for new beginning, new hope to lead a life of righteousness and follow Christ's teaching.

We must remember this message from John 3:16-17 "GOD SO LOVED THE WORLD THAT HE SENT HIS ONLY SON TO THE WORLD, NOT TO CONDEMN THE WORLD BUT THE WORLD MIGHT BE SAVED THROUGH HIM"

Excerpt from my book *The realities of Life.*

SPIRITUAL UPLIFTMENT

If the food, we take nourishes our bodies.

Prayers, meditations and contemplations

Are the tools enriching and uplifting our spiritual souls.

Through these we grow to control our minds and emotions

Thus, bringing us to the next level

Where inner peace and

Satisfaction can easily be achieved.

19

Grieving With The Loss of Your Loved One

Death is inevitable, it does not matter your status in life whether you are an achiever, rich, poor, and famous. All of us will experience the passing of our earthly bodies and the end of life. Most of us fear death, because of the fear of pain, fear of permanently leaving your loved ones, and obsessive fear of unfinished goals. But how about loved ones that were left behind? I believe they too will suffer. Some people will recover in time, but there are those whose lives will be ruined forever, and the consequences will lead to suicide, separation, and mental illness.

Understandably, intense pain and grief will be long lasting, most especially parents losing their child. The sorrow will be forever nested in their hearts. Arguably it is utterly devastating and severe in mourning the loss of your child than the loss of your parents or spouse. One of the most distressing funeral services I had attended was the burial of a child. Beyond words can describe the sorrow and anguish of the parents grieving for the loss of their child. The mother fainted few times and constantly cried and yelled the name of the child as the coffin being transferred into the hearse. It was really the saddest and eerie scene, sending a chill up my spine. I was weeping, and a mother myself I felt the mother's agony.

When the death is sudden and tragic, it will give profound shock to loved ones and often the feeling of parental guilt will prevail thus blaming themselves for the loss of their child.

COPING FOR THE LOSS OF A LOVED ONE

These are my ideas and suggestions; however, the best option is to seek professional help if your grieving is extremely intense.

1. Always remember your living loved ones still need you. They are here for you and will give the love and the strength for you to move on.
2. For people who have strong faith in God, prayers will be the best way to alleviate the loneliness and pain of losing loved one. Trust in HIM will give the spiritual strength you needed.
3. Reach out for organisations that will help you with your present struggle of grief.
4. Focus on your wellbeing, and try hard to get enough sleep, eating healthy balanced diet, and exercising regularly. Your health is the most important thing to cope with the problems you are facing at present.
5. Try to venture different interest and hobbies, to keep your mind away from the trauma you had. You might be surprised to discover your hidden talent.
6. Reach out and start socialising with your friends!
7. Join different community organisations to meet new

friends. There are so many multicultural activities you can be involved.

8   Try to do volunteer work. You can meet different people in all walks of life. It will help you realised that their problems in life might be worse than yours.

9   Read spiritual, inspirational books, and the bible. You can find so many good passages, quotes and messages that can ease your pain.

10 Acceptance....... This is the most important part of grieving; acceptance will lead you to move on. Life goes on regardless. Acceptance does not mean that you had forgotten the loss of your loved one, but recognising the fact that your loved one has left permanently. It is time to be rebuilding your life and tolerate your emotional loss for a positive future in life.

I do hope this quote from the bible Matthew 9:14 can ease the pain of those who lost their child. But Jesus said, "let the children come to me and do not hinder them, for such belongs the Kingdom of Heaven".

Excerpt from my book *The Realities of Life*

In times of troubles, we sometimes question

Our very own existence

In times of mourning, we can find solace,

In the arms of our loved ones

The past can be forgotten, but there are moments,

The memories still haunt us.

No matter how painful it will be.

You must accept things as they are.

Learn to move on

Tomorrow will be another day,

A day of happiness and contentment.

20

My Special Stella Cherry Tree

Live not by the day
But by each moment, each second
Make the most of everything
Each day while living
Because life is too precious
To be wasted away
Lorna Ramirez

Every time I woke up in the morning, I could see through my window sill a lush and healthy cherry tree. This cherry tree gives us each year the sweetest, tastiest and the juiciest cherry, much to our satisfaction especially for my grandchildren who have insatiable appetite for this fruit. Reminiscing the story behind my Cherry tree constantly brings sadness in my heart, thus making this tree so special for me.

It was in the year of 2012, that I rang up the Poyntons Nursery at Essendon asking for information for planting and buying a Cherry tree. I had the pleasure of talking to the owner of the nursery by the name of Warwick. He was so friendly, obliging and spent his time giving me valuable tips for soil preparation for planting a Cherry tree. He recommended Stella, a dwarf and self-pollinating tree.

It took us two weeks to visit the nursery. I inquired for Warwick and the Guy at the nursery informed us that Warwick had reserved the Stella Cherry tree for me. With a sorrowful look on his face, he uttered that Warwick had passed away two weeks ago with Brain Aneurysm. It was so sudden, and he was not even aware he had it. I felt a goose bumped, it was only a week ago, I had double vision, fainted, and found myself in the arms of my husband. The ambulance took me to the emergency hospital. They had suspected a mild stroke TIA (Transient Ischaemic Attack). A complete test was done, everything came back normal. The last test was an MRI (Magnetic Resonance Imaging). From the result they found out I have brain aneurysm, and I was so lucky it did not burst to cause brain haemorrhage, like what exactly happened to Warwick the owner of Poyntons Nursery.

My family especially my grandchildren all love visiting the Poyntons Nursery. They have an amazing collection of plants, shrubs, and trees. I also enjoy visiting their Boulevard Café situated inside the nursery, high on the hill of the nursery overlooking the beautiful Maribyrnong River in Essendon,

What had happened to Warwick and me can happen to anyone. Indeed, I believe we must enjoy each day of our life. We will never know what will happen tomorrow. Kindness, peace, love must always prevail in our hearts. Savour each moment you are with your loved ones. Treat each day as if it is the last day of your life, only then we can appreciate everything around us, and all the blessings bestowed upon us!

Excerpt from my book *The Realities of Life*

Just live for today
What is important is the present
Yesterday is just only a memory
Where the good is to be treasured
And the bad should be forgotten
Make another day of hope and blissful living

21

The Day I Called Australia Home

COMING TO AUSTRALIA

It was raining heavily on that night of the 31st of August 1977, as we drove to the airport for a new life in Australia. My husband is an Electronic and an Electrical engineer in the Philippines, while I am a Chemical engineer. My children were aged 9 and 5. It took us an eight-hour journey from Manila to Australia. I had mixed emotions-excited but scared. We do not know what to expect, going to another country with different culture, no relatives and friends was a huge gamble that time.

Coming to Australia was a part of the Whitlam Government scheme called Assisted Passage Migration, which provided financial assistance to new migrants.

At the airport we were met by the government staff, who led us to a waiting cab.

MIDWAY HOSTEL

We reached our destination at the Midway Hostel at the Hampstead Road, Maidstone, for newly arrived migrants, now known as the Student Village. A friendly staff took us to an interview room where he helped and guided us with our applications for Medicare, Children's allowance, and unemployment benefit.

The board and lodging at the Midway Hostel were free while searching for a job. Once you were employed you have the option to stay for a few months with pay or leave the hostel. They provided us with a two- bedroom unit with a bathroom, toilet but no kitchen. Cooking was not allowed in the unit. Food was provided at the communal or dining hall. Smorgasbord of food, lots of meat, poultry, variety of salads, fruits and desserts were served each meal. At the Hostel there were several communal laundry facilities hence became meeting place interacting and coming to know different races and cultures.

We had a supply of fresh milk and fruit every afternoon. Towels, linens were supplied and washed for our convenience. Sunday mass was given, and a school bus took the migrant children either to catholic or public schools and dropped them back at the Hostel.

Within two weeks both my husband and I had jobs. Filipino families bonded together. The Filipino relationship with each other were quite remarkable, as we tried to hold on to one another for strength and security. At the Hostel, a frail elderly sister assisted us for all our spiritual needs. She also provided us with thick clothing and cardigans for surviving the cold nights in Melbourne.

LIFE AFTER HOSTEL

After two months at the Hostel our family moved to a two -bedroom flat, a walking distance from a Primary Catholic School. Since my husband and I were both working, my heart bled each time I went to work in the morning. Fortunately, we have a Filipino family as neighbour who helped us.

Life in Australia was so different in the 70's. shopping malls, groceries and banks were open only five days a week but on Friday they were open in an extended hour up to 9:00 pm. This was the main reason why we have so many establishments of Milk Bars (a local general stores). You don't' see them anymore. We would barely see a soul when we went to the city during weekend. However, this was compensated for by the fact that almost every weekend, with extended families and friends we went to different camping areas in Victoria- fishing, bush walking and just relaxing.

In the 70's the average loaf of bread was only 48 cents, and the yearly average wage was $9,000 per annum.

During the night, the vacant lot in front of Highpoint mall was used as Drive-In Cinema, very popular at that time. On Sundays, this was used for Trash and Treasure stalls.

In the 70's becoming an Australian citizen was a lot easier. You had to be a permanent Australian residence for two years with a good moral character, the ability to speak and understand English but not necessary to be able to read and write English.

After two years we became an Australian Citizen. We then moved to our very first house.

Years passed the children grew up and finished their university degrees. Now both of us are retired. Hubby and I continue travelling around the world and went to different breath- taking places in Australia.

Our house is just a few kilometres from the Midway Hostel.

Each time I pass by the building, a feeling of sadness, joy, and mixed emotions I felt in my heart. Those unforgettable memories are still in my mind. Our lives and future were shaped and started in this building.

We are so lucky to have given a chance to have a new life in this wonderful country that is AUSTRALIA.

Excerpt from my book *My Innermost Thought*

> In our younger days we were so eager
> To learn new things, venture into new experiences
> Enjoy each time and went through
> Extensive knowledge we so desired
> But it is in our mature ways we can
> Comprehend, understand, and appreciate
> Appreciate everything we have learned and experienced
> Through the years.

22

What I Learned From Covid

Despite the havoc that this Pandemic brings into this world, there are lots of things that COVID 19 made me realised what is important during the time of isolation. It completely changed my perspective in life and learned to appreciate more things I had taken for granted before this pandemic seeped into our lives.

In hindsight, during the isolation, we all had the chance to reflect and analyse the excesses we had before pandemic such as:

- I do not need to buy those extra dresses that just accumulate in my wardrobe
- Those pair of shoes I will only use once
- I do not need those expensive jewelleries that I hardly wear
- Nor, I do not have to have those designer bags that in my opinion are a waste of money
- They are only material things that are not a necessity, and I can live without.
- What matters for me now are health and family
- COVID 19 truly made me appreciate more simple things in life and these are:
- A smile on my face each time I hear the cascading rain

pouring down my roof while falling asleep at night. It denotes breath of life needed by nature and human.
- The children's laughter enjoying as kids, sheer pure innocence and not knowing the perils and sufferings of the present time. The scene of a family gathering eager to see in flesh all their loved ones and interacting with one another.
- The dedication of health workers, scientists working together with love and helping the sick to overcome this invisible enemy we are facing.
- To all the charity volunteers helping those who are needing the most to all people who are doing the right things and adhering to the rules implemented by our government

Indeed, these are the things that made me smile.

I have great hope and positivity with the coming year of 2021. The vaccine will help globally at least controlling this virus that is rapidly without mercy ravaging mankind. For this coming year I wish most of us will still practice the virtue of caring, sharing and looking after with one another. This virus certainly impelled us to be humble, because who and whatever your status in the community you are not immune. This virus does not discriminate

So how about you? What did you learn from COVID 19 and during the ISOLATION?

Excerpts from my book *My Innermost Thoughts*

All of us have gone through several stages in life

Each stage is a learning experience

At the end it is nice to look back

Not counting the years, you have gone through

But counting the special moments That you had been through

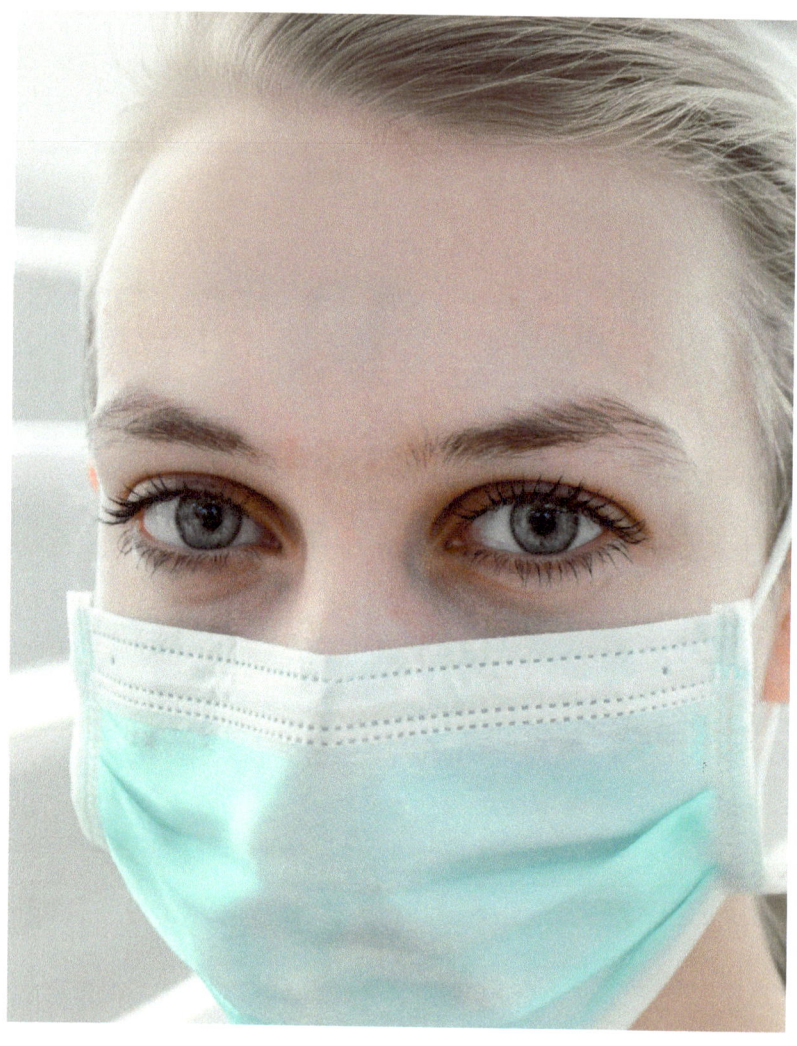

23

For the Love of God

FATHER FORGIVE THEM, FOR THEY KNOW NOT WHAT THEY ARE DOING. Luke 23:34. Today you will be with me in paradise, Luke 23:43. These were the first and second last words of Christ on the cross. Christ humbled himself accepting the will of God to die for our sins. These are the real substance of the meaning of Lent, that is to practice humility and forgiveness as manifested by our lord Jesus Christ.

Lent is the most important celebration and commemoration of the death of Christ on the cross by all Christians around the world. Lent is the 40 days celebrations before Easter (the time of the resurrection of Christ) This is the time for reflections, fasting, repentance, spiritual discipline and most of all forgiveness and humility. After Lenten season, there will be Easter family celebrations, Easter egg hunting, lots of chocolates and sweets. Joyous celebrations for Christ resurrection. For non -believers this is a time for holidays and time off from work. Nonetheless for Christians, no matter how earnest and intense your prayers are, if your heart is full of hate, greed or envy, the sacred time is meaningless.

During the Lenten season countries from different congregation will have their own ways of celebrating. Generally, they make small sacrifices such as giving up certain things they enjoy doing. Some people fast and abstain from eating meat during Lenten Fridays. In the Philippines even though the Catholic church disapproves of performing the penitence, there are people whipping themselves on their backs with bundles of bamboo sticks tied to a length of rope, until their backs will be covered with blood. People are still doing this for repentance of sins.

The Lenten season is also a reminder to all of us that amidst all the suffering and conflict we are going through, there will always be a glimmer of hope, akin to the celebration of Easter, the resurrection of Christ.

According to Matthew 7:23 Christ said "Not everyone who said LORD, LORD will enter the kingdom of heaven, but the one who does the will of my Father WHO is in heaven. "In the realm of religion and Christianity we are encouraged to go to church every Sunday to pray and give homage to GOD. However, there are those who pray often and regularly, yet their hearts are as cold as ice and full of deceit. Will they have a place in Heaven? In contrast There are agnostic, atheist people but their hearts are pure, kind and caring, Will these people have a place in heaven. Indeed these are two extreme examples, but I firmly believe that your actions, the way you treat people, and if you have an inner peace within yourself and others, is what really matters!

HAPPY EASTER TO ALL!!!

Excerpt from my book *My Innermost Thoughts*

Prayers are not the only way to communicate with God

There are other ways, such as a simple act of kindness to others

I am close to mother nature while working in my garden

I can show my appreciation of all the beautiful creations

He had given us

I am a good mother, grandmother, friend and respect for others

Following all HIS commandments and what matters most is following

All that HE preaches. These are more potent ways

Of expressing my love for "HIM" other than prayers!!

23 For the Love of God

24

Welcome ...
The Autumn Season

Thank God it's all over... or is it? It is so refreshing to anticipate the coming of the Autumn season is the transition from summer to cooler months before Winter

The past summer season was devastating. In my forty-one years in Australia, this was the first time I had seen bushfires ravaging so many acres of land, it was unimaginable and calamitous event that this summer's bushfires raged. My heart goes and I can feel the agonising trauma for all those people losing their homes, livelihoods, as they watched helplessly as fires engulfed their properties. My heart bleeds as billions of animals died from this inferno, and for those trees that we lost.

When something happens like this, it brings the goodness in us. So many different community organisations, with different cultural backgrounds, politicians forgetting their differences for the moment are all united and giving, sharing, donating goods and financial support to the victims of bushfires. In Situation like this, we admire especially the firefighters, the volunteers who have tirelessly fought and even risk their lives saving the community.

When calamity like this happens, everybody is equal, being rich or poor does not make a difference, all are going through the same predicament and are at the mercy of mother nature. Encountering such catastrophic event in our life made us realise that nothing is permanent and material things can vanish and are worthless, hence we appreciate more the values of our life.

The coming of the cooler months is gladly welcomed by all of us. At times we do not appreciate things when we have it, only when we lose. Indeed, it will be a sigh of relief that Autumn season is once again here with us.

Sometimes we become more appreciative of what we have now, when we had a traumatic experience, we had gone through such as the Bushfire saga. We started to vision life in a different perspective. Entering the Autumn Season is no difference, we started to look forward for a better tomorrow.

Autumn Season is symbolic for change. The leaves start to fall from the trees, some leaves changing colours. Autumn denotes that in life nothing is permanent, and we should always accept the present. Autumn signifies that we must start looking and preparing for our next phase in our lives

Autumn season is preparing us for the cold months ahead. In the animal kingdom, they start storing foods and some plants and animals preparing for their hibernation during Winter Season

In Autumn we do have lots of activities instore for us. Since the weather is mostly pleasant it is the time to have few day trips with the family to different beautiful places in Melbourne. There are lots of concert, festivities, and multicultural events happening in Melbourne. This is the best time to go camping with friends and families or if outdoor activities are not your cup of tea, you can spend more time gardening because this pleasant weather we have this Autumn Season. This is also the best time to invite friends for a barbecue and why not!

Whatever the season will be, I believe the most important is bonding with families and savour the love of family and friends. After all we do not know what tomorrow brings. So, enjoy life with you loved ones to the fullest

Excerpt from my book *The Realities of Life*

At times hurt is needed

To remind us that we are not as invincible as we perceived

We are

Disappointments are at times essential

To awaken us to the realities of life

That not everything is within our reach

Failures can times act as a catalyst for us to strive more

And can be a tool to open the door for success.

25

Mother Dearest

MOTHER'S LOVE

An excerpt from my book, The Realities of Life

> Giving without expecting in return
> Loving with all thy heart no matter what
> Understanding when others fail to understand
> Supporting in times of sorrow and grief
> And most of all
> Always being there for thy children in every way

Mother's Day celebration will be so different this year. The Inexorable present situation of COVID-19 that we are all experiencing now will have a subdued effect in the way we will celebrate Mother's Day. Nevertheless, it will not hinder us from giving the acknowledgement to the most loved people on earth…
MOTHERS

25 Mother Dearest

The love of a mother is an intense unquestionable feeling, that does not require any explanation at all. Their sacrifices, love, their juggling of their work to care for their children are some of the many of the reasons why Mother's Day should be celebrated.

The bonding of a child started at the womb of a mother. The mother nourishing her unborn child, to make them stronger each day and carrying the child for nine months. After birth, the baby will taste their first precious liquid of life coming from the mother's bosom. Such is a beautiful bond and connection between a mother and child. The love and connection between a mother and a child resonate and manifest not only in humans but also in the animal kingdom here on earth.

I once saw a documentary on TV with a lion who protected her cubs to the extent of sacrificing her life to the predators just to keep her cubs unharmed. An unmistakable act of love of the Lion to her cubs.

As a child whenever we are scared, distressed or anxious, whom do we called first? our mom, of course. Hence this symbolised our trust for her. As a child we found comfort from her hugs and kisses, and I believe that the love of a mother is the greatest and the most powerful love of all.

As we grow up, at times we can be at loggerhead with our mom, we became rebellious and probably we do not realise the hurt we inflicted to her. However, as soon as we have our own family and have our own children, we only then appreciate our mothers.

Let us not only celebrate Mother's Day once a year, but we should also acknowledge our mothers every day of the year, after all once you lose your mother, you lose the best person on earth.

Happy Mother's Day to all the beautiful mothers in the world!

26

Diverticulitis Awareness

Diverticulitis is the most common disorder of the colon in the western population, affecting one third to one half people over the age of sixty. Many are not aware of having this disease since it is usually painless and symptomless. Diverticulitis disease is rare in African villages who have not adopted the western style of eating habits. A simple procedure of Colonoscopy will detect if you have Diverticulitis

I had my first experience of this horrible disease in the year 2008. I have no symptoms or pain.

We were just coming home from visiting my grandchildren when I felt an urge to go to the toilet. I was totally devastated when a huge blood appeared in my stools. An ambulance came and was rushed to a nearby hospital. I was bleeding continuously, and I was given Blood transfusion. Several tests were done including CT scan that confirmed I had Diverticulitis. I was fasting for eight days with no solid foods and only given drips. I stayed in the hospital for twelve days. At present I now watch what I eat, less red meat and more of fruit, veggies, chicken, and sea foods. Hopefully I won't have another attack of Diverticulitis.

WHAT IS DIVERTICULITIS

Diverticulitis is the inflammation of small pouches that is called diverticula, that will develop along the walls of your intestines. It is relatively benign condition called diverticulosis. These pouches can develop at the digestive tract usually at the descending and sigmoid colons. Most people are not even aware if they have the disease.

Diverticulitis can be acute or chronic. An acute diverticulitis can have one or two attacks and inflammation. For chronic diverticulitis, the inflammation and infection may ease but will never heal completely. If left untreated, this can lead to serious complication thus requiring surgery. An infected diverticulitis will affect the adjoining organs such as the large intestine, bladder, and the kidneys.

SYMPTOMS

1. Diverticulitis can be symptomless but at times can have symptoms like those of irritable bowel syndrome (IBS) such as bloating, pain or tenderness at the stomach, alternating diarrhea, and constipation
2. You may also experience nausea and vomiting.
3. Blood in your stool is an indicative of internal bleeding.
4. Fever, chills, and abdominal swelling.

CAUSES

The primary factors in the development of diverticulitis are aging and heredity. For people who are usually constipated, and usually strain during bowel movement, it will create pressure in the walls of the intestine thus diverticular pouches will be filled with faecal matter and some undigested foods. The pouches will be infected leading to the inflammation of diverticulitis.

PREVENTION

1. Having a high fibre diet to have a regular bowel movement.
2. Eating of red meat in moderation
3. Cooked animal protein such as fish, poultry or eggs are recommended.
4. Person with diverticulitis should avoid eating fruit and vegetables with skin.
5. Drink six to eight glasses of water a day to help a regular bowel movement.
6. People with diverticulitis should avoid eating nuts, however some experts do not agree with this.

TREATMENT

For mild attack of diverticulitis, it can be treated at home. However, you still need a physician to make sure you are fully recovered from this. This can be treated with antibiotics and diet modification.

If there is an internal bleeding, hospitalisation will be needed to avoid complications. Intravenous antibiotics will be administered at the hospital. Blood transfusion will be required for massive blood loss. At times surgery will be required if the intravenous therapy failed to work

References...The Medical Advisor Home Edition, Food Your Miracle Medicine, Listen To Your Body

27

Dad ... The Hero

Most of us are fascinated with *super*heroes. Children always have their favourite superhero but their real living superheroes through their eyes are their dads.

The sons perceive their father as an idol, wishing to be like him when they grow up. The daughters when they were young view their fathers as their knights in shining armours ready to help and protect them from everything.

Not all fathers are worthy being good fathers, but generally fathers always love care and are the ultimate protectors of the families, hence they are the strength of a family institution.

Dads are always fun to be with. They play soccer, football and other sports with their children. A father will be there for his family, he is expected to be responsible and carry the weight on all the problems of the family and of course with the help of his wife.

The interactions of the children with fathers during early childhood will develop the children's personalities in their adulthood. His involvement within the family is critical and important to a successful family ties and family bonding.

Nowadays, more and more of mothers are in the workforce, thus the role of the fathers in the 21st century is demanding as ever.

Dads taking huge responsibilities in household works, looking after the children and at times they can do it even better than their wives.

Fathers are expected to be the disciplinarians, but with kindness and softness in their hearts. Quite difficult to be achieved, however as always, they can managed it efficiently and effectively.

All children when they were young enjoyed being sitting on their father's shoulder. They felt tall and loved to see everything around them. This is what fathers do.

Father's love is unconditional. They will always be there for their children, but they do not condone wrong behaviour and attitude. They are firm in their decisions, yet always open to suggestions and ideas. They are willing to accept mistakes, these are the qualities of an ideal and a good father to her children

Father of a Bride, a movie made in 1991, typifies how a father can be overprotective to his daughter. The movie also exemplified how a father feels when his daughter decided to get married and start her own family. A comedy movie but I am sure fathers can relate to this.

So let us acknowledge the real living heroes ... To all the fathers around the world ... Happy Father's Day To You

An excerpt from my book *My Passion, My Calling*

Through the eyes of the children

Their parents are their role models and heroes

Therefore, it is the responsibility

Of every parent to set high standard

To be able to produce

Future responsible adults

28

Planning To Retire?

Retirement is the most crucial stage in our lives. It is dreaded by some, while others are looking forward to it. Are you well equipped and prepared for this?

There are those planning for their retirement in five years or even ten years' time, but sometimes it does not matter how prepared you are. There are some unforeseen circumstances that are beyond your control, such as health issues and death. One must be flexible when these tragic events occur.

Readjustment is one of the key issues taken into consideration when retiring. Suddenly you are with your partner 24/7 hence, it can be quite a shock to both of you. Unfortunately, as a result of these some couples divorces during this time. This is the time for reassessing, compromising, reconnecting with each other. I truly believe that if both people are still in love with each other, this issue will be easily resolved.

Yes, it's true financial freedom helps in retirement. However, there are quite a lot of people who were not fortunate enough to amass wealth leading to retirement. Do not despair, If you have your health, loving and caring families and friends, and you are at peace with yourself and God, happiness is achievable. These are things money cannot buy.

We are fortunate here in Australia, that there are many organisations that help the elderly and retirees. They have monthly events, programs, and entertainment. There are lots of ways to enjoy retirement such as socialising with friends and joining organisations that you have interest in. This is the time to explore your hidden talents, for example learning new hobbies such as painting, photography, volunteering work, writing, and for those who can afford it travelling overseas or visiting beautiful places in Australia.

When I retired seventeen years ago, I had the privilege to look after my grandchildren. It was the most exhilarating experience in my whole life. I also found my passion for writing and music. To date I have published two books and I currently have a third book, a novel, underway. I have returned to studying intermediate piano and have joined several organisations, starting to socialise with friends that I had not otherwise seen in decades!

So, who said that retiring is boring? Not me!

An excerpt from *My Innermost Thoughts*

I was often asked these questions

Are you bored retired?

How do you fill up your time?

I just smile

Because I know within

I'm enjoying every minute being retired.

How can you be bored

sharing every moment with your loved ones?

How can you be bored

exploring, and re-inventing yourself?

How can you be bored

doing the things you're passionate about?

Absolutely my colourful life begins

During my retirement

29

Thanks for the Memories

Each year will come and go, so will be this year. At the end of each year, we are always in the process of preparing, assessing and evaluating the things we had done and had happened in our lives. There are memories that can be forgotten but there are some that can linger on forever and will always makes us happy.

Both pleasant and painful memories can happen for the past year, and for the unfortunate ones, this is the time to move on and try to embrace the coming new year with hope, new life and a new beginning. From the past mistakes we can now set up new goals and aspirations. For grieving families who lost loved ones, remember to concentrate for the living loved ones who still need your care and support.

It is no use having a long list of New Year's resolution. Based on statistic only 8% people will keep their New Year's resolution. Nonetheless remember that the choices we made will create and shape our future.

Be practical and sensible when making a resolution, start with the easiest one, take baby step and when you feel you are ready you can set or aim for your next goal. By doing this it won't create disappointment and frustrations.

Prioritise what is important but consider as well that your changes will benefit not only yourself but your loved ones. Ask you family for support if needed and I am sure they will always be there for you.

I am truly thankful for the memories for this year. It was the year 2017 that we celebrated our 50th wedding anniversary, the same year I had launched my 3rd book and my first novel "Moments of Love, Lust and Ecstasy. The previous year I decided to continue my piano study and fortunate enough to pass the Australian Music Examination Board for intermediate level (AMEB).

This time I won't be making any New Year's Resolution instead I will continue my passion for writing, music and supporting my Charities, most especially The National Breast Cancer Foundation.

Thanks for the outgoing year for all the wonderful memories I have and I hope next year ahead in will be the same or even better for me and for all of us.

HAPPY NEW YEAR TO ALL

Excerpt from my book *My Innermost Thoughts*

It is the choice we make in our lives

That makes life itself

Full of challenges and surprises

Hence shaping and creating

Our journey of life

30

Miracles Do Exist

Each breath we take and each time we wake up are already miracles. Our body is the miracle of life. Cells inside our bodies always change consistently. Different organs interact with each other, each one of them has different functions to give us continuous life on earth. I believe that this is a living proof of daily occurrences of miracles, something beyond our comprehension of the intricate structures of human body.

The vast solar system and how it works, every planet collaborating with one another in a movement in a predictable way, I called that a miracle. To the sceptics, doubters and non-believers, they can always provide technical explanations for this. For us Christians and other religions we strongly believe that there is a greater force that is responsible for all these things to happen.

Is it just only an urban myth when we hear stories of people being cured after praying, or somebody being diagnosed with cancer and given few months to live survive that leaves doctors baffled?

One of the most popular miracles had occurred on the 13th of October 1917, in Fatima Portugal, witnessed by more than hundred thousand of people. It is the apparition of the Blessed Virgen Mary to the three shepherd children. According to the many witnesses after a period of rain, the dark cloud break and the sun appeared as an opaque spinning disk in the sky. It was well documented, and the event was officially as a miracle of the Catholic church in October 13, 1930.

How many times you hear stories of babies falling from a tall building and surviving, would you consider this a miracle?

Excerpt from my book *My Innermost Thoughts*

Who said miracles don't exist anymore?

From the moment I open my eyes each morning

I see the sun shining in the sky

Or hear sound of the rain

Pouring down my roof

I see life in it

Beautiful creations from God

Enjoying the sun

Or feasting from the pouring rain

Crops that we planted

Bearing its fruit

I see miracles in this

Indeed, about the harmonious relationship

Of Nature and Mankind

A Simple thing I can say

Is the miracle of LIFE

31

Forgiveness as a Virtue

The Lord's prayer, a prayer thought by Jesus to his disciples, is now recited by all Christians. A beautiful prayer, very inspiring and a beautiful passage one of which is: Forgive us our trespasses as we forgive those who trespass against us"

How many times do we pray "The Lord's Prayer"? Do we really digest and comprehend the quintessence of its meaning especially the part of forgiveness? Forgiving those who betrayed us, and the degree of harm inflicted on us is not easy, but with sheer determination will be achievable.

By forgiving you can move on and have closure. If there is still hatred in your hearts, inner peace cannot be found, thus it will haunt you forever. People who forgive are happier, healthier and have good positive outlook of life. They are prepared to start a new beginning and the experiences they endured will served as a lesson, making them stronger and be able to face the future with confidence.

There are people who will choose revenge over forgiveness. One form of revenge is not hurting your opponent's physically, but destroying them fall apart emotionally, mentally and spiritually. Will you feel better doing this? I do not think so, you will be worse than ever and you will make the situation more complicated. As the saying goes" a mistake cannot be corrected by another mistake". God's first of His seven words spoken on the cross was *"Father forgive them for they do not know what they are doing"*. Even *up to the* last hour of His death, He was talking about forgiveness. The second time He mentioned forgiveness was during the repentance of a sinner beside Him. A paramount manifestation of the virtue of forgiveness. The world would be peaceful, joyous and better place if forgiveness will always reign in our hearts.

An excerpt from my book

My Innermost Thoughts

Letting it go

Does not mean forgetting the past

It is merely a preparation

For a new beginning

For a new life, for a new hope

Use your past as an inspiration

32

Mother's Unconditional Love

Excerpt from my book *My Passion My Calling!*

A mother's heart is so strong.
It can withstand all the pain, sorrows, and heartaches.
Inflicted by loved ones.
A mother's heart can still withstand and forgives no matter what.
Even there is no more left to give.
One cannot fathom a heart of a mother.
Unless you are a mother.
Lorna Ramirez

The profound love of a mother to her children can never be fathomed, defying logic and reasonable explanations. An example of unconditional love, a love that is full of sacrifices and caring. I firmly believe that our life's journey starts in our mother's womb, carrying and nourishing us for nine months. Then the cutting of the umbilical cord signifies the physical separation of a mother and her child. However, the baby still needs nourishment, hence the milk of the mother symbolises life for the newborn. This is an unmeasurable bonding between a mother and the baby. A face that only a mother can love is a popular expression and an example of a mother's unconditional love.

The influence of a mother to her children is indeed significant. Well-loved children are mostly self-confident and have a positive outlook of life. In the animal kingdom, animal moms protect their young by shielding their bodies and keep their young safe from predators. In the recent stabbing attack at the Westfield Bondi junction in Sydney, a mother desperately tried to protect her nine months old baby from the perpetrator at the expense of her life, truly epitomises a mother's love to her child.

HISTORY OF MOTHER'S DAY

Mother's Day originated back to the ancient Greece celebrating the Goddess Rhea, who was the Goddess of motherhood, fertility, childbirth, and comfort of good living. The festival of Rhea does not take place anymore in Greece. However, the Greeks are still celebrating Mother's Day and is very similar to America's Mother's Day celebrated on the second Sunday of May.

Anna Harvis in America started the official celebration of Mother's Day tradition after the death of her mother in 1908. She wanted to celebrate all the sacrifices that mothers give to their children. President Woodrow Wilson signed a declaration of Mother's Day in 1914, declaring the second Sunday of May to be a national holiday to honour mothers.

Constance Pens wick Smith created Mothering Sunday movement in the United Kingdom between 1910 and 1920. She was inspired reading the article in 1913 about Anna Jarvis, an American woman residing in Philadelphia who started Mother's Day in the US. Then Smith linked the concept of Mothering Sunday, as a Mother's Day celebration. The UK Mother's Day celebration is different to that of the US. The UK Mother's Day celebration is in the fourth Sunday of Lent while the US is on the second Sunday of May.

REASONS FOR CELEBRATING MOTHER'S DAY

Celebrating Mother's Day is one way to acknowledge the manifestation for all the sacrifices, unconditional love and support mothers give to their children. This is also one way of the glorification of motherhood. In my opinion motherhood is the noblest job of all. Mothers are responsible in shaping the characters of their children emotionally and spiritually. Celebrating Mother's Day, we recognise their important roles in the family. They act as doctors, financials, disciplinarians, moderators and many more.

Celebrating Mother's Day is one way for us to reflect the love, compassion of mothers and for us to remember and appreciate that motherhood is the most demanding job requiring patience, strength, and dedication to their families. As always, the task of mothers will never end.

Suffice to say, because mothers are the most loved people in the world it is truly justified that Mother's Day should be celebrated every year and possibly every day of the year. ONCE YOU LOSE YOUR MOTHER, YOU LOST THE BEST AND LOVING PERSON IN YOUR LIFE!

33

It's All About Love

My own true love, my own true
At last, I found you, my own true love

This is the theme song from 1939 epic romantic movie "Gone with the Wind". This movie was set during the time of the American civil war. The main character characters of this film are Scarlett O'Hara, Rhett Butler, and Ahsley Wikes. The movie is all about love of the country and an unrequited love. Scarlett is deeply in love with Ashley who is in love with someone else. Nonetheless, Scarlett decided to marry Rhett for her own convenience, hence the start of conflicts in their marriage.

WHAT IS LOVE

Love is an emotion. It cannot be seen but can be felt with intense passion and deep affection. Love defies logic, and even science can only define love with limited perspective.

Based on science, mutual attraction is divided into three categories: Adrenaline, Dopamine and Serotonin. These are the chemicals secreted by the body each time we have exciting experiences in our lives. Science can identify all these, however reasons for falling in love with a person is a mystery.

According to Dr Helen Fisher who is an expert in Biology of love and attraction, she said love can be broken down into 3 categories: Lust, Attraction and attachment. A set of hormones are responsible for each category of love.

In my opinion, the best kind of romantic love will be an attraction with an attachment. Loving someone involves commitment, sacrifices for well-being and happiness for your loved ones. It entails supporting them in the darkest moments in their lives. Putting your own needs to the side, thus showing them, you care for them regardless. Loving someone is encouraging loved ones to be strong. Making them feel important and showing your unconditional love in every way you can. Indeed, these are the real essence of the power of love. These small price to pay to feel the glory and bliss of loving and being loved.

Surely this kind of love can be manifested to a friend, to your children, to a soldier's devotion to their beloved country, health workers dedications to their jobs and so on.

THE PERILS OF LOVE

A euphoric feeling of being in love can create havoc in many ways. Friends, families can be divided because of love. Suicide and in some cases, murders are the aftermath of the cruel effect of love.

Quintessentially the intensity of the pain of loving is at the utmost level when loved ones goes to eternal sleep. It will leave a gaping hole and for others the pain will be forever. At times it would take time to heal, and for others the pain will be forever.

Unrequited love will cause heartaches and sorrow as exemplified by the film, Gone with the Win. Rhett did everything to win the heart of Scarlett. He is married to her, but for her heart always yearns for Ashley. Rhett had enough, confronting and telling Scarlett he will be leaving her. Scarlett realised her mistakes and pleading to Rhett that she will change and ask for a second chance. At times we are blinded failing to see someone who loves and will always care for us dearly. Once this love disappears it will be gone forever As Rhett is about to open the door to leave, he saw Scarlett crying and pleading not to leave her. Rhett ignoring and unmoved he delivered a very powerful line

"Frankly my dear I don't give a damn"

**Excerpts from my book
"Reflective Contemplations"**

Finding Love

Being in love we start
TO rediscover our inner self
And the real meaning of what
Life is all about
Finding love is magical
Moments and precious time
We shared with someone
We truly love and adore
Finding love is priceless

34

What's in a Dream

ST. Matthew 1:20

"But while he thought on those things, behold, the angel of the Lord appeared unto him in a dream, saying, Joseph, thou son of David, fear not to take thee Mary thy wife: For that which is conceived in her is of the Holy Spirit"

This is one of the many documented dreams in the old and new testaments. Werner Nell, from the school of Behavioural Science in South Africa, stated that dreams were a source of Inspirational insight and a prophecy from God. He then emphasised that a dream is a way God interact with people. Some are symbolic, and they are those, with instructions from God.

There are many theories about dreaming and various explanations as to the reasons why do we dream. Experts in dreams and scientists believe that a dream is our brain responding to the biochemical changes and electrical impulses occurring while we are sleeping. They have also said that a dream is an extension of our past and present experiences while we are awake.

According to Facthacker.com, there are eight different kinds of dreams: daydreams, Lucid dreams, nightmares, recurring dreams, healing dreams, prophetic dreams, signal dreams, and epic dreams. However, some believe that there are only two kinds of dreams: God's dreams, and man's dream. In God's dreams the setting, atmosphere, style, themes are so vivid and clear that it will have a great impact and forever be embedded in your memory. In man's dreams it is usually disorganised, disjointed, and waking up you don't know what the dreams were all about and they don't have a significant impact on you.

MY GOD'S DREAM EXPERIENCED

In the last few months, I prayed fervently, that God will give me a sign if I proceed of having a brain aneurysm procedure by the first week of November 2019. On the 2nd Sunday of August between 2;00 to 3:00 am, suddenly out in a blue without warning, in my dream, appeared a bearded man wearing a very white robe at the door of my family room. His hair was at shoulder length. As I gazed at His face, I felt a strong thump, as if someone struck a heavy blow to my chest. My whole surroundings turned white, and the man was glowing with a face so white because of the reflection of the light. His left arm was on his heart, and the right arm was outstretched towards me. His face was so beautiful, serene and calm, then I felt the joyous feeling of peace and contentment at that very moment. His piercing eyes was so intense that I started talking in different languages. At this point my husband who is agnostic, woke me up and said I was talking in a language he cannot comprehend. I hugged my husband, and sobbed, we both had goose bumps

The following day I talked to a Pastor in Melbourne, and he commented and explained to me that what I described was documented in the bible and it was the son of God, Jesus who appeared to me in my dream. He also added that even though I have a good heart He is reaching for me to have a strong connection with Him and that is the only way to enter the kingdom of heaven. I had never read a bible before, and I am doing it now.

I also talked to a priest in Melbourne, he suggested that I must write and document my dream., to inspire Christians and non-believers. He also stated that I should be happy only a handful of people had seen Christ in a dream. But why me, I am not religious and not worthy of it.

On October 5 of this year, I went to my neuro- surgeon to get my latest Brain MRI result. My specialist was surprised that my brain aneurysm had shrunk and said that there is no need for a human intervention. Is this just a coincidence, is this a miracle? For sceptics and non-believers, they would say that my body heals itself because I do have a healthy lifestyle. For Christians, they believe it is a miracle. Whatever the reasons maybe, I strongly believe that I was cured because I still have a mission. God wanted me to continue writing inspirational messages and reach out for those people needing the most. How about you…… Do you believe in Miracle?

Excerpt from my book *My Innermost Thoughts*

Who said miracles do not exist anymore?

From the moment I open my eyes each morning

I see the sun shining in the sky

Or hear the sound of rain

Pouring down my roof

I see life in it

Beautiful creations from God

Feasting from the pouring rain, the crops that we planted

Bearing its fruit

I see miracles in these

Indeed, about the harmonious relationship of nature and mankind

A simple thing I can say

"Miracle of Life'

What's in a Dream Inspirational Photo

It's All About Love Photo

35

The Spirit of Christmas

Where there is love, kindness will prevail, where there is kindness, there will always be forgiveness. This is one of my unpublished quotes.

I truly believe that these three virtues of Love, Kindness, and Forgiveness are the real spirit of Christmas. Most of us will always think of Christmas as the period of holidays for overseas and interstate, functions, parties and bonding with families and friends. There is nothing wrong with these celebrations. However, this Christmas we should contemplate the true essence of Christmas which are the flowing:

LOVE John 15:12 "This is my commandment that you love one another as I have loved you". Love can be manifested in many ways: love for your parents, children, spouse, friends, country, and the list go on. All kinds of love have one thing in common: commitment and sacrifices. It is very difficult to love everyone, especially your enemies, and those who betrayed your trust and hurt you. Try not to hate them, and instead pray for them, so you can achieve inner peace. It is so easy to love the lovable, very easy to accept people who share our own belief and conviction. It is easy to love our families and friends, however it will take a lot of courage to love and accept people who are different, the unlovable. I believe that the world would be a peaceful place to live if we accept and respect everyone regardless of gender, race, religion, and other differences.

KINDNESS This is the virtue of being considerate, friendly, generous, and empathetic to the feelings of others. Kind persons are always willing to help others, who are in need, without expecting anything in return. Kind people are not judgemental and accept a person as they are. Unfortunately, there is a misconception that they are weak, but the truth is they are caring and compassionate towards people.

One of the best ways of celebrating Christmas is doing something good for others. A simple act of kindness can make a difference. This is good for our body, mind, and spirit. Saying comforting words to people suffering physically and mentally, visiting a friend at the hospital giving them positive thoughts and telling your friend that you care and will pray for her immediate recover are only some of the examples of an act of kindness.

FORGIVENESS When we forgive, we will be able to free ourselves with anger, hence it will be the start of healing our inner selves and the beginning of the process of moving on. We cannot achieve peace of mind and contentment without practising the virtue of forgiveness.

Matthew 18:21-22 then Peter come to Jesus and asked, "Lord how many times shall I forgive my brother and sister who sins against me? up to seven times?" Jesus answered, "I will tell you not seven times but seventy-seven times."

Based on Matthew 18: 21-22, this is an inspiration to follow what Jesus said and this Christmas we should start soul searching and have the courage to forgive those people who had offended you. It will be a slow process of healing, but at the end and with sheer determination we will be able to do it triumphantly.

We must not forget that God so loved the world that he gave his only son, so that everyone who believes in Him will not die but will have eternal life……. John 3:16

Excerpt from my book *Reflective Contemplations*

In Love we rediscover
Our inner selves
And the real meaning
Of what life is all about
Love teaches to be humble.
Love teaches us to be forgiving
To be sensitive and to be compassionate

Lorna Ramirez   www.lornasbook.com

Quotes and Inspirational Messages

1

It is not all about the quantity of years spent in your life. It is all about the quality of years you live will matter

2

I believe that the main purpose of life is not all about yourself. It is all about helping others and importantly how will you be able to use your talent not only for your own benefit but for the good of mankind.

3

Live not by the day, but by each moment, each second. Make the most of it, because life is too short to be wasted

4

If things did not happen your way, it is probably not meant to be. Time to be flexible and move on. There will always be a silver lining ahead. The present alternative will be much better than the first one.

5

Once or several times in our lives

We make crucial decision

That can change the path of our lives

This what I called

Challenge

Without challenge and risk

We cannot improve our lives

Hence realisation of our dreams

Will be out of reach

6

Regardless of what you are now

Do not forget the people

Who had helped

When you are down

7

Be always yourself

No pretence or hypocrisy

Always stay true to your values in life

8

One must not change or sell your soul

Just to achieve your dreams

9

Do not give up your dreams

Keep on chasing

10

If you believe you are always better than the rest

Inner conflict will follow

And peace within cannot be achieved

11

The more talents and blessings you have

The humbler you should be

12

To some people happiness and joy can be achieved

By caring and helping others especially those

Needing the most

13

Comparing yourself to others

Will deprive you of the joy of living

Insecurity will prevail ending up

To a miserable

Way of life

14

Some people will take more than they should

While some will give, more than they have

Indeed, these are the two kinds of people on earth

Which one are you?

15

Miracle do exist

Look around you

And you will know the reason
Waking up
each day is already a blessing

16

A modicum of honesty and truth
Will be needed if you are not willing
To expose the truth

17

A life filled with memories of loved ones and friends
Will be a life full of joyous blessings

18

Generosity is opening your hearts to all
Who are needing the most
Regardless of who they are

19

Embracing the realm of life
One should always be flexible
To avoid frustrations

20

It does not matter how old you are
Changes in life are inevitable
Learn to adjust and be flexible

21

Humility and renunciation

Of greed, power, will find peace

Within

22

A song in my heart will always praise

The glory of God

23

God given talents, should be used

To serve and share

And not only for self-gratification

Humble people are not affected

With fame and glory

Instead, they inspire others

And transcend their virtues

For the goodness of mankind

25

Just because you are well learned

Does not make you a better person than the rest

It goes more than deeper than that

26

It is in giving and sharing

That some people can comprehend

And find the joy of living

27

It is in what we believe that makes us strong

To fight for a worthy cause

No matter will be aftermath

28

Be wary for those who sympathise for you

At times they do the exact opposite

And bringing you down without your knowledge

29

Other people weaknesses

Can help us fathom our own frailty

Thus, helping us to improve our strength

And the betterment of ourselves

30

At times we are blinded by the truth

To protect our own self vested interest

31

Life is not simple

At times it is complicated

Learn to be flexible and accept

Things that cannot be changed

Just enjoy life while you can

32

Do not be too trusting

People will see it as a weakness

They will start to use you

For their own benefit and interest

33

With the blessings and graces from God

I will continue to reach, touch people's heart

Through my inspirational writings.

34

Any cause is worth fighting for

If it is for the benefit and interest

Of Mankind

35

People will defy the truth

Once ego and interest

Will be at risk

36

It is your choice to do your own legacy

A choice between right and wrong

A choice between good and evil

37

Cherish the life you live

Cherish loved ones and friends

They give us strength

And reasons for living

38

Good intentions, no matter how sincere it is
Will be at times misinterpreted
Harsh reality of life

39

Your beliefs and convictions
Will truly define who you are

40

Words once spoken
Can be forgiven
But never be forgotten
Like a sword piercing through the heart

41

At times we see things
Not what they really are
But the way we want them to be

42

In a group, unity can never be achieved
If there are egos, greed and vested interest

43

Contemplation is a tool
To help the mind to go to the next level
Of awareness and peace of mind
To know what is right, and what is wrong

44

A humble reminder: There will be always someone
Better than you

45

A life filled with love
Is a life, full of happiness and bliss

46

Within the realm of my own experience
Human minds and emotions
Are difficult to comprehend

46

A heart filled with bitterness and despair
Will not find peace within themselves
And peace with others

47

The false mysticism by some of us
Who believe that only prayers can lead us to salvation
Often produces ersatz form of hope and expectation

48

To be humble is to be
Simple and truthful

49

I wish we all can be free for the love of money
Avarice, greed, these are slowly creeping
And suffocating our lives

50

At times love hurts

But I would rather be hurt

Then not to love at all

51

Peace within can never be achieved

If you always think

You are superior and better than others

52

Our talents given to us

Are not solely for yourself

But to share with others

To make a difference in this world

53

Yes, you can forgive

But you cannot forget

Akin to a wound that can be healed

But the scar will always be there

54

You cannot enter to the deepest centre

Of your soul

Unless you practice the virtues

Of love, selflessness and compassion

55

I must be a lucky person

Not in terms of wealth and material possession

But by being surrounded with loving families

And caring friends

56

I want to be remembered not by who I was

But what I was during my living years

57

Afraid to face our own shadow

Can hinder us to progress and move on

58

Love is beyond comprehension

No one can find the answer to how

And why we fall in love

Really a mystery

Beyond the concept of science

59

At times what you see

Are not really what they are

At times it is only an illusion

We should scrutinise, analyse, what lies

Beneath the surface

60

What makes us humble
Will be the best gift of all

61

The best way is stay away from toxic people
They will drag you to a dark pit of obstacles

61

Mere words are not enough
Your actions will show what
And who you really are

62

It is not about how much you have in sharing your blessings
At times there are those who just had enough
Yet they love to share
More than those who have more than enough

63

Sinners will be the absence of love
Their world will be filled up
With hate, deceit, betrayal and greed

64

Happiest I am
When surrounded with loved ones
And real caring friends

65

A love that flows from your heart

Without pretence

Will be the greatest gift you can give

66

A person with a good heart

Can see the beauty on everyone

And not being judgemental

67

It is your choice

It is your decision

Do not blame others for your failures

Take responsibility for your actions

68

Realities of life... The influence of friends and environment

Are at times stronger than families and loved ones

69

A heart filled with love

Is a heart filled with joy

Contentment and peace within

70

We should profess compassion, understanding

Love and unity

With this trying time,

we are facing now COVID 19

71

The very essence of any relationship

Are trust and respect

Once gone

Relationship would be at stake

72

Greed, deceit, hungry for power

Are the worst enemies of mankind

73

Mistakes and experiences

Are the best mentors in life

74

The best virtue is doing charity solely

For the services for the community

And not for your own self-vested interest

75

There is nothing more important to me

Compared to the love and care of my families and friends

The rest are only secondary

76

Anticipation often creates frustration

77

Amidst the anguish

You can be able to appreciate more

Your blessings in life

78

Let not the bitter memories from the past

Overshadow your hope, goals, and aspiration

For the present and the future

79

COVID 19! Puts a break on every one of us

It evaluates what is important to our lives

Redirect and focus sensibly what is relevant

Thus, helping us the right path as we walk

The journey of life

80

Relying on each other's support and strength

One of the lessons learned during COVID 19

81

We became more appreciative for the things we have

During this Pandemic, compared to pre-COVID 19

82

The hurt is deeply felt

Once you realised your mistakes and shortcomings

83

How quickly your perspective in life change

Once unforeseen circumstances

Crossed your path

84

At times we do not know how and when to stop

Once greed, fame and power

Overtaken the heart and soul of a person

85

Your thoughts and emotions

Are the ultimate

Quintessence of your soul

86

When the music stops

The laughter vanished

This is the time

You will know who your real friends are

87

When there is love

Kindness will prevail

When there is kindness

Forgiveness will come easily

Hence peace within and

Others will be easily achieved

88

In the twilight years of your life
It is good to look back through the years
And then realised what life is all about
You know now what you do not know before

89

At times we can see the beauty and the positivity
On each negative aspect
We had encountered

90

We are only temporary residence here on earth
We, loved ones, and friends will be gone one day
So, cherish each moment, each day while living

91

I believe silence, and meditations
Are the best therapy in life

92

What is in a kiss? A kiss so tender but filled with love
A kiss so sweet that envelops my body and soul
A kiss so caring and saying "I love you"
Indeed, the very essence of the power of a kiss

93

To be perfect is to be imperfect
Imperfection makes you humble
And a catalyst to aspire
For all your dreams to come true

94

Reading between the lines

Is a fascinating way

To discover the real thought of a person

95

Thinking that you are better than anyone

Will lead you nowhere

And no prospect to succeed in life

96

Of course, I do have several disappointments and frustrations

But all of these, make me a stronger person and help me shape

My perspective in life

97

Sadly, we can only plan our future

And everything will favour our way

We should not be disappointed

If things gone wrong

Learn to be flexible and move on

98

Mental and emotional abuse

Are more lethal, than physical abuse

99

Denial is your utmost enemy and hindrance

For your success, progress, and growth

Though it is quite difficult to change

Do one step at a time

Until you succeed

100

One of the reasons

We abhor others

Is because we can

See through them

Our own inner weakness

That others don't have

101

One should always be strong

And follow your beliefs and convictions

Failing to do so

Will haunt you forever

In your life

102

We always mourn for

The loss of loved ones

But no one mourns

For the loss of one's soul

103

Just a simple smile

A warm hello and gracious thank you

Would make anyone's day

Very special

104

It is up to us to relinquish the past

Then let it go and move on

Failing to do so

We become prisoner of ourself

And peace within

Can never be found

105

Quest for knowledge is never ending

The desire for adventure, calculated risk

Are the spices of life

106

To do an act of kindness

Yet there are people who chose

To inflict pain, and misery to others

107

There are times when we want

To leave away from our past

But our past never leaves us

Keeps on haunting us

Wherever, and whenever we are
And it is up to us to accept
And deal with it courageously

108

When love is too intense
The hurt will be deeper than ever

109

At times hurt is needed
To bring us back to our senses and sanity
To be able to realise
That not all our heart's desires
Will come true

110

I believe in this saying:
Things happened for a reason
Those people we met that
Created an integral part in our lives
Those heartaches and frustrations
That make us a stronger and a better person

111

The most beautiful words are yet to be spoken
The most sweet-sounding melodies are yet to be heard
The most soulful and romantic songs are yet to be sung
But all these are still embedded in one's hearts
Ready to set free

112

The expression of your eyes

Your body language

Can reveal your thoughts and emotions

More than the words spoken

113

The vision of happiness to some

Will be the accumulation of wealth and power

But for me it will be the triumphant

Raising of law-abiding successful children

And a life filled with the love of families

And caring friends

114

At times silence

Is more powerful

Than words

115

Imperfection is not abhorrent

Imperfection makes us humble

Imperfection drives us to work harder

Inspires us set goals

To achieve the pinnacle of success

Also by Lorna Ramirez...

ISBN: 9780646975412

Available from Amazon and other online outlets.

ISBN: 9780648213000

Available from Amazon and other online outlets.

ISBN: 9780648213024

Available from Amazon and other online outlets.

ISBN: 9780648213048

Available from Amazon and other online outlets.

ISBN: 9780648213062

Available from Amazon and other online outlets.